PSYCHOLOGY & THE CHURCH: CRITICAL QUESTIONS...CRUCIAL ANSWERS

FOR NEARLY TWO THOUSAND YEARS prior to the rise of modern psychiatry and psychotherapy, the church has ministered to believers experiencing mental, emotional, and behavioral problems by using the teachings of the Scriptures and in the power of the Holy Spirit.

Contemporary Christianity's embrace of psychology, then, raises an important question: Was there an insufficiency on the part of God's Word and His Holy Spirit during those two millennia that made it necessary for the church to turn to modern psychotherapy in order to more effectively address a Christian's problems of living?

Answering that question is the focus of this program, which considers carefully the influence of psychological counseling upon the church. In the history of contemporary Christendom, no secular enterprise has had such a profound influence on Christianity as has psychological counseling. The critical question raised by these developments is: Have they been helpful or harmful to the body of Christ?

T.A. McMahon, co-author of *The Seduction of Christianity*, is your host for this ground-breaking documentary. Featuring perspectives and insights of both Christian and secular experts including Dr. Martin and Deidre Bobgan, Dr. Tana Dineen, and Dave Hunt, this powerful presentation exposes the roots—and results—of Christianity's embrace of the beliefs of Freud, Jung, Rogers, Maslow, and others. Produced by The Berean Call. About 55 minutes *(DVD only—not available on VHS)*.

THIS GROUND-BREAKING DOCUMENTARY ADDRESSES KEY CONCERNS:

- *In the last fifty years, multitudes of pastors have added clinical counseling degrees to their theological credentials.*
- *Psychological theories have been preached so often and from so many pulpits that they are accepted without question by increasing numbers of Christians as biblical doctrines.*
- *The Christian church in the United States has become a major referral service for clinical psychologists and psychiatrists.*

About The Berean Call

The Berean Call (TBC) is a nonprofit,
tax-exempt corporation which exists to:

ALERT believers in Christ to unbiblical teachings and practices impacting the church

EXHORT believers to give greater heed to biblical discernment and truth regarding teachings and practices being currently promoted in the church

SUPPLY believers with teaching, information, and materials which will encourage the love of God's truth, and assist in the development of biblical discernment

MOBILIZE believers in Christ to action in obedience to the scriptural command to "earnestly contend for the faith" (Jude 3)

IMPACT the church of Jesus Christ with the necessity for trusting the Scriptures as the only rule for faith, practice, and a life pleasing to God

---

A free monthly newsletter, THE BEREAN CALL, may be received
by sending a request to: PO Box 7019, Bend, OR 97708; or by calling

1-800-937-6638

To register for free email updates, to access our digital archives, and to
order a variety of additional resource materials online, visit us at:

www.thebereancall.org

PORTRAIT
OF AN
ADDICT
AS A
YOUNG MAN

PORTRAIT
OF AN
ADDICT
AS A
YOUNG MAN

A Memoir

BILL CLEGG

LITTLE, BROWN AND COMPANY
New York Boston London

Little, Brown and Company
Hachette Book Group
237 Park Avenue, New York, NY 10017
www.hachettebookgroup.com

First Edition: June 2010

This book is a work of nonfiction. The names and descriptions of some of the people in it have been changed.

Little, Brown and Company is a division of Hachette Book Group, Inc. The Little, Brown name and logo are trademarks of Hachette Book Group, Inc.

Library of Congress Cataloging-in-Publication Data
Clegg, Bill.
    Portrait of an addict as a young man : a memoir / Bill Clegg.
        p. cm.
    ISBN 978-0-316-05467-6
    Int'l ed. ISBN 978-0-316-09768-0
    1. Clegg, Bill.   2. Drug addicts — United States — Biography.   I. Title.
    HV5805.C595A3 2010
    362.29092 — dc22
    [B]   2009024014

10 9 8 7 6 5 4 3 2 1

RRD-IN

Printed in the United States of America

For everyone still out there

Think of light and how far it falls, to us. To fall, we say, naming a fundamental way of going to the world — falling.

— WILLIAM KITTREDGE, *A Hole in the Sky*

Contents

CONTENTS

PORTRAIT
OF AN
ADDICT
AS A
YOUNG MAN

Scrapers

I can't leave and there isn't enough.

Mark is at full tilt, barking hear-it-here-first wisdom from the edge of his black vinyl sofa. He looks like a translator for the deaf moving at triple speed — hands flapping, arms and shoulders jerking. His legs move, too, but only to fold and refold at regular intervals beneath his tall, skeletal frame. The leg crossing is the only thing about Mark with any order. The rest is a riot of sudden movements and spasms — he's a marionette at the mercy of a brutal puppeteer. His eyes, like mine, are dull black marbles.

Mark is squawking about a crack dealer he used to buy from who's been busted — how he saw it coming, how he always does — but I'm not paying attention. All that matters to me is that we've reached the end of our bag. The thumb-size clear plastic mini zip-lock that once bulged with chunks of crack is now empty. It's day-break and the dealers have turned off their phones.

My two dealers are named Rico and Happy. According to Mark, all crack dealers are named Rico and Happy. Rico hasn't shown up the last few times I've called. Mark, who makes it his business to know the day-to-day movements and shifting status of a handful of dealers, says Rico's Xanax habit has resurfaced and is begin-ning to slow him down. Last year he didn't leave his apartment in Washington Heights for three months. So for now I call Happy, who shows up after midnight when the $1,000 limit on my cash card zeroes out and I can start withdrawing again. Happy is the more reliable of the two, but Rico will often deliver at odd hours when the other dealers won't. He'll come in the middle of the day, hours late but when the rest are asleep and closed for business. He'll complain and give you a skimpy bag, but he'll come. With Mark's phone, I dial Rico's number but his voice mail is full and not accepting messages. I dial Happy's and it goes straight to voice mail.

Happy and Rico sell crack. They don't sell cocaine to be inhaled, pot, Ecstasy, or anything else. I buy only bags of precooked crack. Some people will insist on cooking their own — a tricky operation that involves cocaine, baking soda, water, and a stove top — but the few times I tried this, I wasted the coke, burned my hands, and ended up with a wet glob that was barely smokable.

Give me the scraper, Mark barks. His stem — the small glass tube packed on one end with Brillo pad wire — is caked with residue, so after he scrapes it out and packs the end again, we can count on at least a few more hits. He folds his legs in a spidery arrangement and for a moment appears as if he will tip over. He looks like he's in his sixties — gray-faced, wrinkled, jutting bones — but claims he's in his early forties. I've been coming to his apartment for over three years, with increasing frequency, to get high.

I pass him the craggy metal strip that had until last night been the support behind the nylon web of an umbrella. Scrapers come from all sorts of things — wire coat hangers mostly, the ones without paint; but umbrellas have long thin metal strips, sometimes hollow half cylinders, that are particularly effective at cleaning out stems and generating a miracle hit or two when the bag is empty and before the need comes to check the couch and floor for what I call crumbs, what Mark calls bits, but what all crack addicts know is their last resort until they can get another bag.

I reach toward Mark to pass him the scraper and he flinches. The stem slips from his hands, falls in slow motion between us, and shatters on the scuffed parquet floor.

Mark gasps more than speaks. *Oh. Oh no. Oh Jesus, no.* In a flash he's down on all fours picking through the debris. He rescues several of the larger pieces of glass, brings them back to the coffee table, lays them out, one by one, and begins picking and scratching at them with the scraper. *Let's see. Let's see.* He mumbles to himself as he maneuvers frantically over each shard. Again, his joints and hands and limbs seem animated not by life but by strings pulling and tugging him—furiously, meticulously—through a marionette's pantomime of a fevered prospector scrabbling through his pan for flecks of gold.

Mark finds no gold. He puts down the scraper, the bits of glass, and his movements come to a halt. He collapses back into the couch, where I can practically see the strings that held him aloft now glide down around him. The bag is empty and it's six a.m. We've been at it for six days and five nights and all the other stems are destroyed.

Morning glows behind the drawn blinds. Minutes pass and nothing but the low whine of the garbage trucks outside cuts the quiet. My neck throbs and the muscles in my shoulder feel thick and tight. The throbbing keeps time with my heart, which slams in my chest like an angry fist. I can't stop my body from rocking. I watch Mark get up to begin sweeping the glass and notice how his body rocks with mine, how our sway is synchronized—like two underwater weeds bending to the same current—and am both horrified and comforted to recognize how alike we are in the desolate crash that follows when the drugs run out.

The creeping horror of these past few weeks—relapsing; leaving Noah, my boyfriend, at the Sundance Film Festival nearly a week early; e-mailing my business partner, Kate, and letting her know that she can do what she wants with our business, that I'm not coming back; checking in and out of a rehab in New Canaan, Connecticut; spending a string of nights at the 60 Thompson hotel and then diving into the gritty crackscape of Mark's apartment with the drifters there who latch onto the free drugs that come with someone on a bender. The awful footage of my near-history flashes behind my eyes, just as the clear future of not having a bag and knowing another won't be had for hours rises up, sharp as the new day.

I don't know yet that I will push through these grim, jittery hours until evening, when Happy will turn his cell phone back on and deliver more. I don't yet know that I will keep this going—here and in other places like it—for over a month. That I will lose almost forty pounds, so that, at thirty-four, I will weigh less than I did in the eighth grade.

It's also too soon to see the new locks on my office door. Kate will change them after she discovers I have come in at night. This will be weeks from now. She'll worry that I might steal things to pay for drugs, but I'll go there only to sit at my desk a few more times. To say good-bye to the part of me that, on the surface anyway, had worked the best. Through the large open window behind my desk, I'll look out at the Empire State Building, with its weary authority and shoulders of colored light. The city will seem different then, less mine, farther away. And Broadway, ten stories below, will be empty, a dark canyon of gray and black stretching north from 26th Street to Times Square.

On one of those nights, before the locks are changed, I'll climb up into the window and dangle my feet, scooch close to the edge and hover there in the cold February air for what seems like hours. I'll crawl down, sit at the desk again and get high. I'll remember how excited everyone was when we opened nearly five years before. Kate, the staff, our families. My clients—novelists, poets, essayists, short story writers—came with me from the old literary agency, the place where I'd started as an assistant when I first came to New York. They came with me, and there was so much faith in what lay ahead, so much faith in me. I'll stare at all the contracts and memos and galleys piled on my desk and marvel that I once had something to do with these things, those people. That I had been counted on.

On Mark's couch I watch my legs shake and wonder if there is a Xanax in his medicine cabinet. I wonder if I should leave and find a hotel. I have with me my passport, the clothes on my back, a cash card, and the black NYC Parks & Rec Department cap I recently found in the back of a cab, the one with the green maple leaf stitched on the front. There is still money in my checking account. Almost forty grand. I wonder how I've made it this far; how by some unwanted miracle my heart hasn't stopped.

Mark is shouting from the kitchen, but I don't hear what he's saying.

My cell phone rings, but it is buried under a pile of blankets and sheets in the next room, and I don't hear that either. I'll find it later, the voice mail full of terrified calls from friends and family and Noah. I'll listen to the beginning of one and erase it along with the rest.

I won't hear the tumble of the new locks on the door of the apartment where Noah and I have lived for eight years — how the sound has changed from a bright pop to a low click as the bolt flies free while his hand turns the new key for the first time. I can't hear any of this. Cannot feel any of these things that have happened or are about to as the construction that was my life dismantles — lock by lock, client by client, dollar by dollar, trust by trust.

The only thing I hear as Mark angrily sweeps the glass from the floor, and the only thing I feel as the city rustles to life outside, are the barking demands at the end of the marionette strings. Through the endless morning and the crawling afternoon hours, and after, they grow louder, more insistent; tug harder, yank rougher, shake the cash card from my wallet, dollars from my pockets, loose change from my coat, color from my eyes, life out of me.

Cheers

It's January 2001 and Noah's cousin Letty is giving a small dinner at her brownstone in Brooklyn Heights to celebrate the launch of the small literary agency my friend Kate and I are about to open. Letty is a well-bred daughter of Memphis. Wellesley educated, widowed, and much younger-looking and acting than her sixty-something years, she has the bright, smiling, good-hearted eagerness of an underdog. Unlike her supersleek, wife-of-a-former-ambassador sister, Letty has always seemed slightly at odds with her privileged upbringing. She hasn't needed to work a day in her life, but she talks often about her jobs in the design departments of several book publishers and her many years working for foundations. She has two daughters, Ruth and Hannah, and scads of girlhood friends with names like Sissy and Babs whom she often flies back to Memphis to celebrate birthdays or anniversaries with. Letty is one of the kindest people I have ever known.

It is the end of January, one week before the agency officially opens. We don't have phones, stationery, or bank accounts. I'm anxious that we still have to hire an assistant and a bookkeeper, but I'm more anxious that we will not have money to pay either. Noah and I arrive at Letty's ten minutes late, and Kate and her husband are already there. Letty has arranged for someone to take coats, serve drinks, pass hors d'oeuvres, and attend to the dinner table. He's in his mid- to late thirties, Asian, attractive, clearly gay, and a bit too friendly. His name is Stephen and his flamboyance makes me self-conscious in the presence of Kate and her husband, whom we haven't socialized with as a couple much and who seem now, together, very straight.

Stephen asks Noah and me what we'd like to drink and scampers off to the kitchen. He brings us two glasses of white wine, even though I asked for a vodka and Noah a Scotch. He flusters and apologizes and goes back to the kitchen but does not return. Five or so minutes pass and Letty gets up to look for him. A few minutes later he comes out with the drinks. Letty is clearly embarrassed.

The evening is decadent. Caviar, shrimp, and cheeses before dinner, then roast lamb. I have too much of everything and am full long before dessert is served. Noah and Letty both give toasts — both have tears in their eyes as they do. I shift uncomfortably in the beams of their praise and cringe, not for the first time, at how close I am to a cousin of Noah's and barely know any of my own. At how Noah and I will go to weddings and birthdays of cousins and siblings and nieces of his and I see my family once a year — at Christmas usually — and then for only a day and a night.

On the way to the bathroom, I ask Stephen to bring me another vodka. He forgets and I drink more wine. As I finally catch a gentle buzz, I look around the table and wonder how on earth I ended up here. Nights like these are for other people, people like Kate and Noah who — with their Ivy League degrees and supportive families — seem born for toasts and congratulations. At dessert, instead of drinking the port Letty has Stephen open, I get up and fix another vodka. Stephen sees this, realizes that he never brought me the earlier one, and from then on is very quick to refill my glass.

Noah and I hold hands in the cab ride home. I've had seven or eight vodkas, at least as many glasses of wine, and still feel a few drinks shy of where I'd like to be. I think of all that is left to do in the coming weeks to open the agency, and of the two other parties being thrown to celebrate. One is a cocktail party at the new apartment of a friend of Kate's; the other is a seated dinner for fifty or so clients and publishing colleagues hosted by my friend David, who is also one of the first writers I worked with. I worry that I'll need to address the crowds at both of these parties — say something at least by way of thanking the hosts — and I begin to think about how to make sure I won't have to. I close my eyes and try not to focus on how much I want to call Rico and do a few hits. After four or five drinks, this option usually rises up and floats in front of me until I either call him, call another dealer, or fall asleep.

It's just before midnight, and my mind starts racing with ways that I can break away from Noah and score. A manuscript left at the office? Cash I need to get from the ATM? Nothing seems plausible. As we cross the Brooklyn Bridge back into Manhattan, Noah takes both my hands and tells me how proud he is—of me, of the agency. As he speaks, the lights from the bridge flicker across his scruffy beard, kind eyes, longish sideburns and close-cropped, receding hair. I lean into him and away from the other thoughts. He smells the way he always smells—like Speed Stick deodorant and fresh laundry. I relax a little, think for a moment that there's not so much to worry about, that everything will work out.

Getting into bed that night, I remember Stephen, the guy at Letty's, and how he forgot to bring out several dishes warming in the oven, spilled a glass of wine, and made flirty eyes at me through dinner. I wonder how Letty found him and remember his lingering too long at the table, asking too many questions, and seeming oblivious of his mistakes. I remember that he let us know he went to Princeton and that, when it came up that Noah was a filmmaker, he listed all the famous people he knew—playwrights, activists, actors. I also remember his writing his number down on the back of a napkin and pressing it into my hand when I went into the kitchen for a glass of water; how he held my hand a beat too long when he told me that he'd bartended lots of book parties, that I should call him sometime. And though he'd been a disaster all evening, I know, as I fall asleep that night, that I will.

Over a year later, when Stephen is setting up a small table in our TV room with glasses and ice—something he has now done for us at least half a dozen times—I notice a long burn mark down the side of his thumb. I ask him what happened and he stops what he's doing, looks at me as if he's been waiting for me to ask this question for a long time, and says, *You don't want to know.* But I do know. Addicts have antennae that can sometimes detect the kindred frequency of other addicts, and in this instant I pick up Stephen's. In fact, I've probably been responding to it since the second we met. But it's not until now—when I know exactly how he burned himself—that I fully understand the reason I hired him, why he is now in our apartment working another party, even though he has twice stood us up on the day of an event with some complicated excuse of illness or family trouble. And so I say, *Maybe you need to be more careful what you smoke,* and when he smiles and asks, *Are you?* I know that this will lead to something. That the ball is in play. I'll be amazed later when I remember what I say next. *Not as careful as either of us should be.* And then next: *We should set that up sometime.*

I throw a party at the apartment when Noah is out of town. It's a Thursday night and I've already cleared the decks so I don't need to go into work the next day. All evening I pretend to be tired—yawning and stretching, rubbing my eyes—hoping to encourage people to leave early. I imagine the first hit and the bloom of exquisite calm it will bring and I quietly, invisibly, detest everyone in the apartment for being there. I move through the apartment with my seltzer—what I always drink when I organize anything larger than a dinner party—and as I'm talking and smiling and hugging congratulations and thank-you-for-comings, I'm running down the list of things left to do. Check in with Noah to give him the sense that the night has wound down and I am heading to bed. Run out to the cash machine to get Stephen $300—maybe $400—to go wherever he needs to go to score. I'll also need at least $300 to pay him for bartending, since he accepts cash only. I decide to tell him not to bother cleaning up, that I'll do it so he can get going.

Stephen leaves around eleven fifteen and returns after one. I've just finished breaking down the bar, washing the glasses, and putting away the sodas and napkins. (He'll include those two hours on his bill.) This night is important. Not because it's the first time I sleep with him. Not because I spend another $700 I barely have. But because at some point, around four in the morning, when we have smoked nearly through the bag, Stephen calls his friend Mark, who, in a few swift minutes, is at the door with more.

Mark is a restaurant publicist. Tall, neat, angular. I notice right away how he vibrates. As if some electrical charge shocks through his body at a low but steady thrum. I also notice how he speaks to Stephen. Like Fagin to the Artful Dodger, he has some authority over him, and even though it's clear he's on his best behavior, I can see how their dynamic involves some commingling of brutality and care. As Mark holds up our stems and complains how oily and burnt they are, Stephen flutters around him like a nervous nurse attending a surgeon. Mark gives him a you-should-know-better look and shakes his head. Stephen doesn't tell him that they're burnt because of me. That I have, as I always do, scorched each stem with hits that pull too long and flames that are too high. Everyone I ever smoke with will complain about this. And though I will try, each time, to inhale as gently as I can, it always seems like I'm not pulling hard enough, as if the flame is too low, as if I'm not getting enough.

At some point after Mark arrives, Stephen stops speaking to me directly. There seems to be some new rule that Mark is the only one who can address me, and when he does, he is wildly polite, overly complimentary (the apartment, my looks). It's as if I'm in the forecourt of a long con, and instead of feeling hesitant or cautious, I'm thrilled.

The night grunts on until ten or so the next morning. Stephen and Mark amble out into the day, and by Saturday night I have invited them over again. By Monday morning, my bank account is empty and Mark has suggested he and I get together on our own sometime that week. Noah calls a dozen or so times, and I let the landline ring, turn the cell phone off, and don't call him back. On Monday afternoon, my assistant comes into my office and says Noah is on the line, upset and demanding to speak to me. I close the door, and he cries on the other end of the line and asks me to please stop. Could I just please stop. I feel awful and tell him of course and I'm sorry and that it won't happen again. He presses for details and I get mad. Amazingly, he apologizes. I throw Stephen's number away. I throw Mark's card away. But it doesn't matter. Both call over the next weeks and months, and at some moment, I can't remember exactly when or which one, I write a number down. And at some other moment, not long after, I call.

First Door

It's time to go. He's had to pee for hours, but it's always the last thing he wants to do. The problem — that's what his parents call it — *the problem* is that if he goes, meaning, to the bathroom, he won't actually be able to go. In the way he describes it to himself then, it hasn't *built up enough* yet. There isn't enough pressure. He will wait a little while. Wait until dinner is over, when no one will notice if he's gone for too long. Sometimes it takes as long as an hour. Sometimes he can't do it at all. And sometimes it only takes a few minutes. He never knows until he's there.

It's after dinner and he's standing in front of the avocado green toilet. Noises happen behind the closed door — a dropped ice tray, cursing, breaking glass, louder cursing, a phone ringing. The house swells with urgency. From somewhere inside these sounds, a voice that will always remind him of wind chimes calls, *Billy, are you all right?*

Billy ... , his mother calls again, but her voice fades.

Nothing for a few moments. Just the green toilet. Hurry, he thinks. Hurry. His hands work furiously over the end of his penis. A loud knock at the door. Then two. A different voice. His father's. *Jesus, Willie, don't make a career out of it in there.*

Little-guy cords—usually navy blue, sometimes green—bunch at his feet. Fruit of the Looms wrinkle just below his knees. He's been in there for over half an hour. He's come close at least three times, but each time it doesn't work. Doesn't happen. He knows it's going to sting—like bits of glass trying to push out—but he just wants it over with. He shuffles in front of the bowl—left, right, left, right—and squeezes the end of his penis. Rubs it with both hands. The pressure builds and his brow is sweating. He has a terrified sense that if his parents find out, there will be trouble. His father has told him that he has to stop taking so long in the bathroom. When he asks his son why he jumps around and makes such a big production of it all, the boy doesn't have an answer. *Cut it out* is what his father tells him, and he wishes he could.

He runs the water in the sink to cover the sound. The shuffle becomes a dance, the kneading becomes a fevered pinching. From a faraway room he hears his older sister, Kim, crying. His father yells her name. A door slams. His mother calls out. A kettle of boiling water whistles from the kitchen. None of these sounds have to do with him. But someone—he can't tell who—is knocking at the door now. Just knocking, no voice. The boy is a panicked animal—jerking and jumping and pinching before the bowl. He braces for another knock. There is more shouting from down the hall. The sound of something breaking. His hands, his legs—his whole body riots around the pressure at his middle. He's sure his parents can hear him, convinced they will come bursting through the locked door at any moment. He tries to stop the jumping but he can't. It feels as if the whole house—his parents, his sister, the cats, the whistling kettle—has gathered on the other side of the door.

In a moment—the one he's desperate for but can't create—none of it will matter. In that moment, he won't hear the slamming and banging and yelling. As the stinging pressure crests and his body flaps away from him, he won't hear anything. In that streaking moment when he loses control and everything fades out in a flash of pain and relief, he will spray the wall, the floor, the radiator, himself.

He doesn't see any of the mess until the little oblivion passes and he's able to steady himself and direct the pee into the bowl. He aims toward the back to avoid the ruckus of water and it goes on forever. He sees there's a big clean-up job to be done, and he's already anxious about what to say when he's on the other side of the door. Once he's finally finished peeing, he begins pulling yards of toilet paper from the roll, spools that ribbon around his feet and begin to soak up the pool of urine on the tile. He wipes down the toilet and the walls behind and to the side. He gets on his hands and knees and begins sweeping the damp away in long wide arcs. He pats his pants down with the tissue until it pills and crumbles in his hands. He puts too much toilet paper in the bowl and it clogs and the water rises. He knows to put his hand up the drain and yank the paper free to avoid another mess. He plunges his arm in, tugs frantically at the clog, and, like an answered prayer, the bowl empties. Just as this happens the knocking begins again and now it's both parents at the door. His pants and underwear are still bunched around his ankles. He hasn't pulled them up yet because he knows that beads of blood have sprung up at the tip of his penis and it will take a few dabs of tissue and a minute or two for it to dry before it's safe. Often he rushes through this part and will have to throw his underwear out later as little brown spots of blood bud and dry in the white fabric. He's tried stuffing toilet paper in there, but it usually slips to the side and doesn't work. Sometimes he forgets and tosses the underwear in the hamper and sees the dryer-dried briefs folded and spotty in his dresser drawer days later. His mother never says a word to him about the briefs, about the peeing—about any of it. This has been going on for as long as he can remember. He has no memory of standing at a toilet and peeing when he wants to.

What are you DOING? thunders from the other side of the door. His father again. The boy calls out that he is coming, just a minute. He mutters to himself—*Please God, please*—actually, he's been muttering this to himself since he locked the bathroom door over forty-five minutes ago. He will never be more specific in his plea. His pants and shirt are soaking with water, with urine. He pats himself down one more time with a wad of toilet paper and puts it in the wastepaper basket under an empty tissue box and a used toilet paper roll. He wipes everything down, again, just one more time — the radiator, the bowl, the toilet seat, the floor. He scans the room again for signs of his time there. He wipes, with his hand, the sweat dripping from his brow and pats his hair carefully into place. He breathes in, murmurs another quiet prayer, turns off the light, and hopes the light in the hall is off so his soak-stained clothes aren't obvious.

He calms his breath, palms the doorknob, and braces for what's on the other side. He is five years old.

Flight

Snow is falling outside the Holland Tunnel. Cars aren't moving. Horns sound and drivers yell. My flight to Berlin is scheduled to take off in less than an hour, and there is no way I'm going to make it. Noah is already there, having arrived at the Berlin Film Festival directly from Sundance to show his film two days ago. I call my assistant, who booked a four-o'clock car for a five thirty flight, which I only now realize isn't enough time, particularly with the snow. It is, of course, not his fault, but I tell him it is and that my life is about to change, and not for the better, as a result. I hang up. These will be my last words to him, to anyone in my office.

I have nearly a full bag—three medium-size rocks and a scattering of crumbs—in my pocket. A clean stem and lighter, wrapped in a kitchen towel, are wedged somewhere in my L.L. Bean duffel bag, between manuscripts, a pair of jeans, a sweater, and a pile of Kiehl's products. The driver is a young, deep-voiced Eastern European woman, and I've already sung her my if-you-only-knew-how-important-it-is-that-I-get-there-on-time song to persuade her to work some kind of magic and levitate us past the traffic. She just stares at me through the rearview mirror. I wonder if she can see how strung out I am, how far over the line.

I know this is going to be the last straw. Even if Noah forgives me again, despite the fact that he knows I've been using since I left him at Sundance, Kate will not. I've been out for almost two weeks and canceled three meetings with her to go over our long-avoided partnership agreement and finances. I have told everyone—friends, clients, employees—that I have thrown my back out and am going to doctors, acupuncturists, and masseurs. But the truth is that since I got back from Sundance five days early, I've been rattling around the apartment in a thick cloud of crack smoke. I've left the building only a few times, to run across 8th Street to the cash machine and next door to the deli for lighters and Brillo wire. The liquor store has made daily deliveries of Ketel One, and I've called the housekeeper to tell her I'm home sick and not to come.

At some point before getting in the car, I send Kate an e-mail telling her to do what she needs to do, that I've relapsed and that she should protect herself in whatever way is necessary. Before I press Send, I look out the window at the thick flakes of snow coming down in slow motion between the buildings and think I am doing her a favor. Giving her permission to get out and move on. But

I feel next to nothing as I end our partnership, our business, my career. I regard that nothing the same way you observe a cut on your finger just after accidentally slicing it with a knife but seconds before the blood appears. For a moment it's like looking at someone else's finger, as if the cut you made has not broken your skin, the blood about to flow not your own.

I finally get to the airport and race ahead of the line to the first-class counter. The woman there tells me right away that I've missed my flight. I ask her if there is another and she tells me there is one that goes through Amsterdam in three hours. Without hesitating I buy a first-class, full-fare ticket. I have over $70,000 in my checking account at this point, and I think, barely think, that five or so thousand is nothing. I ask her if there is a hotel at the airport, because I want to lie down and rest before my flight. She looks at me and pauses before telling me there is a Marriott a short cab ride away. I thank her, check my bag through for the seven-o'clock flight, and take my ticket. In the cab, I call Noah and leave him a message that I missed my flight — *The traffic was terrible*, I say in mock frustration — but I'm booked on the next one out.

The cabdriver is a handsome, dark-eyed Hispanic guy, and I immediately strike up a conversation. How I get to the moment when I ask him if he parties, I don't know, but I get there. He says yes and I say, *With what?* and he answers, *Beer and pot*. He asks me with what and I come right out and tell him. He pauses and asks me if I have any on me and I say yes. He asks if he can see it and, without hesitating, I reach into my pocket, pull out a rock, and hold it up between the two front seats. He slows the cab, eyes the drug seriously, but says nothing. When I pull it back, he laughs and tells me he's never seen it before, and I ask if he wants to hang out. He tells me sure, later, after his shift, and gives me his cell phone number. I take it, even though I know my flight will take off before he's done. He doesn't say his name so I look at the driver's ID framed in Plexiglas behind the passenger seat and notice that it's obscured by a piece of newspaper. I ask him his name and he mumbles something inaudible. I ask him again and he says what I think is Rick.

Something in his manner shifts as we pull up to the Marriott. He suddenly cools, and I'll remember, later, that he barely asks for the fare, that when I hand it to him, it seems irrelevant. I hardly register this, since I'm preoccupied with how lucky it is that I missed the flight, that I now have a few hours to get high.

I get to the room and shut the door behind me as if I'm closing the curtain on a great, terrifying stage where I've had to perform a grueling part, the skin of which I can now finally shed. I take off my coat and pack a big hit. Crumbs scatter on the bedspread as I hold the stem up to light, but I don't care. I pull hard and hold the smoke in for as long as I can. When I exhale, the stress of the last few hours disappears and in its place swells a pearly bliss.

I soon become aware of my body and feel restless in my clothes. I take my sweater off between the first and second hits. They seem like part of a constricting costume for the performance on the other side of the door and of no use now. By the third hit I'm naked, though I grab a towel from the bathroom and tie it low around my hips. I will always do this when I get high. I will always think my torso looks lean and muscled and sexy. I will always, many times, clock myself in the mirror and think, Not bad. I will remember some version of the lines from Ben Neihart's novel *Hey Joe*, when the narrator checks himself out in the mirror and thinks smugly that he's *keeping his shit tight*. I will, to be perfectly honest, turn myself on.

I scooch the towel lower down my hips, cinch it a little tighter, and begin to get restless for company. I call the number of the taxi driver but no one answers and it doesn't click to voice mail. I do this thirty or so times in the next hour. I put what's left of the bag in an ashtray and thrill to what seems like an endless amount. I'm sloppy as I pack these hits. The bedspread and floor are soon speckled with crumbs. I know that at some point I will be on my knees picking them up, trying to tell the difference between crack crumbs and other debris. There will never be a time when I smoke crack that doesn't end with me on my knees, sometimes for hours—hunched over carpets, rugs, linoleum, tile—sifting desperately through lint and cat litter and dirt, fingering the floor, like a madman, for crumbs. I know this is where it will end up. As I pack those lazy crumb-scattering hits in the beginning, I will, each time, think of the floor like a retirement account. Little bits neglected into a place where I will seek them out later. It will comfort me to know there is somewhere to go when the bag empties, something to do while I'm waiting for the next delivery. But in the beginning, in the abundant beginning, this will always seem a long way off.

In the room at the Newark Airport Marriott, as in most rooms where there is crack, porn flickers on the television. This time it's straight and soft and on Pay-per-view. I pay for all six movies and flip between them as one scene disappoints or dulls. I have drunk the small bottle of white wine, the two beers, and both small bottles of vodka from the minibar by the time I realize I need to get back to the airport and onto the plane. Since there is still a large pile of drugs left in the ashtray, I wonder whether I should go at all.

But I do. I let my stem cool and wrap it in a wad of tissue paper. I gather the two rocks and the remaining crumbs from the ash-tray and put them back in the mini zip-lock they came in. I ditch the towel, scramble into my clothes, and shove the pipe, bag, and lighter into the front pocket of my jeans. I scan the room a dozen times. Clean every surface and pick up whatever crumbs I can from the floor. I unpack the bag and pipe and lighter at least three times to smoke just-one-more-hit before leaving, to get just the right high to face the lobby and the airport. I leave less than an hour to check in and get on the plane. Noah has called three or four times, but I have not picked up, nor have I listened to his messages.

I don't bother checking out. I go straight to the taxi stand and get in the only cab there. The driver is a big black guy — fat but muscular, linebacker-style. Forty, maybe fifty. The stem, still hot from heavy use in the room minutes before, burns in my jeans pocket like a little oven. Of course I ask him if he parties. He says he does, and I ask him if he ever smokes rock. *Sure do,* he says, and right then, within the first minute of getting into the cab, I know that I am not getting on the plane. That I will probably never make it to Berlin.

So let's hang out, I say to the linebacker behind the wheel, and he says, *Sure thing.* As we edge up to the Continental departures drop-off, I tell him to head back to the hotel, that I'll catch a later flight. He doesn't question or hesitate, just pulls away from the terminal and says, again, *Sure thing.* I call Continental's 800 number and tell them I'm sick and can't make the flight and could they transfer the ticket to the next night. Unbelievably, they can and they do. I am booked in a first-class seat the next night at eight. Acres of time, a bag of crack, company lined up, and a hotel less than a minute away. I've just missed two flights, e-mailed Kate and relinquished any say or stake in our agency, tossed my career down the chute, and stood up my beloved and no doubt frantic boyfriend. I've done all these things and I couldn't be happier.

I leave a message on Noah's cell phone saying they canceled the second flight and that I will be flying out tomorrow. I speak slowly and calmly, with just a little can-you-believe-it annoyance so as to seem normal and not high. Once I've left the message, I turn the phone off so that I don't have to hear it ring when he calls back.

Later, the taxi driver and I sit in his cab behind a 7-Eleven some-where in Newark. He's anxious about being seen in the hotel because he picks people up and drops them off there every day. I pack his hit—small because there is precious little left—and as he lights up, I tell him how horny I get when I smoke. He nods in agreement as he exhales, and soon zippers come down—mine first, then his. I take a hit and he holds himself and talks about his wife, how she blows him but never wants to fuck. I inhale so hard that I burn my forefinger and thumb. I should be over the Atlantic right now, I think, but instead I'm behind a 7-Eleven, in the shadow of a Newark, New Jersey, overpass. What I want is the blurry oblivion of body-crashing sex, and instead I get a gloomy jerk-off session without enough drugs to get either of us high. As the bag empties, I start to feel shaky and it occurs to me that I've gone nearly a week without sleep. It's ten thirty p.m. and my flight tomorrow evening isn't until eight. I ask the taxi driver if he knows where to score more and of course he doesn't. I hide one last rock in the small front pocket of my jeans so there will be something when I get to the hotel room. I start thinking about whether I should go back to the city—to Mark's, or to a hotel somewhere in Manhattan where I can call Happy. But the city seems time zones away. And if I go there, I know there will be no turning back, no chance of making it to Berlin.

The taxi driver drops me off at the Marriott, and I call Happy the second I get to the room. After much haggling, he agrees to drive out to the hotel, but only if I will spend at least $800 to make it worthwhile. I say no problem.

It is just after eleven when Happy and I speak. At eleven fifty he calls me from the parking lot to say he's there. I can't remember his ever delivering this quickly in Manhattan. I leave the room, take the elevator down to get cash from the ATM in the empty lobby, walk as slowly and calmly as I can, past the check-in desk and out into the parking lot, where his red minivan idles. My heart slams in my chest and my throat is so thick with fear I can barely speak as I hop into the front seat. Happy, as usual, is wearing his white sweatpants and plain black hooded sweatshirt. The only thing missing are the large earphones that usually ring his neck. He's Dominican, in his early thirties, and we never say much to each other beyond amounts, addresses, and number of stems. He is always calm, and even though he's driven all the way out to an airport hotel from Manhattan, tonight he's no different. His movements are slow and patient as he counts out the sixteen bags, and he asks no questions as he hands me two clean stems. I shove it all in my front two pockets, thank him for coming out so fast, and head back to the hotel.

If anyone had stopped to watch me go to the cash machine and withdraw stacks of bills, several times because of the $200 transaction limit, then head out to an idling van with tinted windows, and return minutes later with bulging pockets, it wouldn't take much imagination to understand what had just transpired. As obvious and sloppy as I know the whole operation is, I know that once I get back to the room and take a big hit off one of the crystal-clear new stems, everything will be okay. That all the grim and alarming truths barking loudly around me will vanish in a blast of smoke.

And so they do. It's one o'clock and I have a spectacular pile of crack in the little ashtray on the nightstand. This is the most I have ever had on my own, and I know I will smoke every last bit of it. I wonder if somewhere in that pile is the crumb that will bring on a heart attack or stroke or seizure. The cardiac event that will deliver all this to an abrupt and welcome halt. My chest pounds, my fingers are singed, I fill my lungs with smoke.

Bringing Down the House

He's six. Diminishing the value of the house. That's what he's being told. Bringing it down with piss-splattered heating vents in the bathroom coated with rust and stink. Making it more difficult to sell by scrubbing the pattern off the wallpaper next to the toilet each time he sprays there and tries to clean it up.

They are in the green Volkswagen, and it's not the first time his father has told him these things. That his piss is costing the family thousands of dollars is a fact as old as memory. He is quiet, as always when his *problem* comes up. His father talks in sharp, lean bursts that usually end with *C'mon, Willie. Just get it together,* or *Jesus, kid, fix it.* And then long stretches of silence. The only sounds in the car are the low hum of 1010 WINS on the radio and the click of his father's pipe against his teeth.

They are on a highway heading home from Boston. They drive uncomfortably fast until the traffic congeals and the swearing and the steering wheel pounding starts. As his father turns the radio down and adjusts the heating vents, he imagines him before the great panel of lights and gadgets in the cockpits of the planes he flies. The ones filled with passengers who trust him to take them across the ocean, to London and Paris. There are times—like this—when he can't imagine anything his father cannot do.

The traffic gets worse and his father grumbles at the cars in front of him. The boy stays quiet. He's relieved that the attention has shifted away from him, from the reason they are in a car together today. They have gone to see a doctor—the one the Boston Red Sox use, his father said—to find out what exactly is wrong with him.

What precisely goes on at this doctor's office, he will forget. Maybe he remembered in the car, ran it over in his head as they rode home, or maybe it had already slipped away. In any case, he will spend years trying to remember, but the only part that ever comes back will be the car ride itself. He'll remember the old lines about wrecking the house and the strange, nearly sexual air of the day—so much talk about penises and pissing. Something clandestine and shameful about the whole trip, which had begun with his mother's pinched announcement at breakfast that he and his father would be going to Boston to visit a doctor. He'll remember how worried she looked and how far away. He'll remember wishing the car would rattle at high speed right off the road and go up in a blaze. He will persist with that kind of wish for years — in school buses, planes, vans, trains. He'll also remember — and this most vividly — a prediction his father makes. That very soon his friends — Timothy, Derek, Jennifer — and their parents will stop letting him into their houses for sleepovers or playdates. That it's just a matter of time before they catch on, and once they do, there will be no way they'll allow such a mess, such a monster, in their houses.

This last bit will stick. It will expand into a belief that they already know and are complaining to his parents and warning their children, his friends. He'll worry, until they move away a few years later to a smaller town farther north and deeper in the woods, that secretly his friends and their families and even his teachers know about his problem and that there will come a day when they'll make a spectacle of that knowing. He will imagine and sometimes think he'll hear them say *monster* under their breaths.

And so they drive. His father presses on with talk of declining house values, promises of banishment. The radio mumbles low on the station that will still, years later, remain for him the source of the gloomiest, most desolate sound, and be the station playing in every car his father owns. As they get off the highway and begin to snake along the winding Connecticut roads toward home, there is silence and the occasional click of pipe against teeth. The world outside seems to be in on all of it: the trip to the doctor and the warnings afterward part of some long-considered, collectively agreed-upon plan of action. *There is nothing physically wrong with you,* his father eventually shouts, exhausted no doubt by the whole day. *It's just a matter of willpower. Of choice. God only knows what kind of permanent damage you're doing down there. What kinds of things you won't be able to do, later.*

This last part must have been said on the way up the driveway or sitting in front of the garage because he will remember hearing the word *damage* as he looked up at the charcoal-colored ranch house, knowing that a new radiator and fresh wallpaper were nothing compared with what would be needed to fix him.

Complicated Theater

There is a bar in the Newark Airport Marriott. It's almost midnight and I phone the front desk and find out that last call is at one. I shower and shave and clean up as best I can before going down for a drink and company. I put in a new pair of contacts because when I'm getting high, no matter how much water I drink or how many eyedrops I empty into my eyes, the lenses dry up and pop out. I have packed four boxes of contacts for this trip, and since I've been in the hotel, I have already replaced the left one once and the right one twice. I know I will have to be more careful but as with everything else — drugs, money in my bank account, time — at this point there seems more than enough to last. I wear my navy cashmere turtleneck because it's thick and cabled and hides my rickety frame; it is also expensive and, I think, obscures the cracked-out truth of me. I wear my jeans, and even though I am now cinching my belt to its last hole, I still need to tuck the front of the sweater in to keep them from falling down. I know I will have to find a leather shop in Berlin to punch new holes.

Once I get dressed, I pace through the routine of taking a hit, guzzling a glass of vodka, going to the mirror to make sure I look okay, messing with my hair until I give up and put on the Parks & Rec Department cap. I start to get warm and a little horny and restless in my clothes, and I take my sweater off, lie down on the bed, turn on some porn, and jerk off. I wallow in the little patch of dizzy pleasure for a few minutes, and as it fades and I pour another vodka to cut the speedy buzz and mellow out the high, I think, Just one more, a big one this time to kick up my courage. And so one more. I put my sweater back on, fuss in front of the mirror, squeeze a few eyedrops in, pat down my hair, put on my cap, yank on my jeans, and before I know it I'm on the bed again, shirtless and shimmering and enjoying the short while before I need my stem, another drink, and just a little more time before I leave the room.

I finally make it downstairs to the bar and am immediately disappointed that the place is nearly empty and dotted with a few couples and business colleagues traveling together. I don't see the vulnerable and restless loner I'm looking for—that magical kindred partner in crime, game for a long night.

I slam three or four vodkas and begin to get shaky. More than twenty minutes without a hit is pushing it, and I've been downstairs for at least half an hour. Vodka usually eases that jittery feeling, smooths the little wrinkles of horror that slip in as a high teeters toward a crash, but it's not helping much now. In any case, I've got the largest pile of crack I've ever seen waiting in the room and there is no good reason to stop. I signal the waiter as calmly as I can, leave two twenties and a ten with the $35 tab, and make for the elevator.

The night swirls with thick smoke, and I go through nine of the sixteen bags by early afternoon. I have never smoked so much in such a short time — two bags, shared with at least one other person would normally be a big night — and my skin tingles with heat and I'm aware of every breath and every heartbeat. All my clothes and toiletries are scattered around the hotel room and still I have too much left to smoke to make leaving the room seem like a good idea. I call the cabdriver from last night and leave a dozen messages. He doesn't call back. It takes hours to pack and clean up, with hundreds of pit stops to smoke and drink along the way.

With three hours before the flight, I finally make my way down through the lobby. As I check out, I notice, near the door, five or six men between the ages of forty and sixty. Each has some distinct but unspecific quality — gray slacks, grim shoes, Windbreaker. Head-to-toe JCPenney. They mumble to one another and it seems — though it's not exactly clear — that they all have earpieces with wires tucked discreetly into their shirts. There is no one else in the lobby. Only one cab waits at the taxi stand. I hear, *That's him,* from one of them, or I think I do, as I make my way through the electric doors to the breezeway outside. As I get into the taxi, I notice all five or six of them leaving the hotel and heading toward two or three cars parked in front of the building. The driver gives me a knowing look and states more than asks, *Continental*, which is of course my airline, but how does he know? I ask him and he says, *It's Newark, everyone flies Continental.* I look at his ID displayed in the Plexiglas partition and see that the photo, just like the one in the cab yesterday, is obscured by a piece of cardboard. I begin to panic. He starts the car, pulls away from the hotel, and as I watch the cars filled with the JCPenney guys follow us, I know I am, right now, crossing over from one world into another. I can already imagine myself remembering this cab ride, how it will signal the end of the time when I was free.

I'm about to be arrested. I have a bag of crack and a very used pipe folded in tissue in the front pocket of my jeans. I don't see how I can get rid of it. Throw it out the window? No, these guys, whoever they are, are right on our tail. Stash it in the garbage when we pull up? No, same reason. Stuff it in the seat cushion of a car that is probably being driven by an undercover DEA agent? Obviously no. Swallow it? Maybe. But the glass pipe . . . what do I do with the glass pipe? These solutions flash and burst, one by one, again and again, as we crawl toward the terminal. None are possible.

Before I left the hotel room, it seemed like a good idea to bring along enough crack to get high in an airport bathroom just before getting on the plane. As the terminal comes into view, I realize, too late, how insane this idea is. We pull up to the drop-off zone and

I notice that one of the cars is directly behind us. I look away as I get out of the cab and pay the driver, who seems indifferent to the fare.

As I make my way into the building, my only thought is when. When will they tap my shoulder and ask me to empty my pockets and open my bags. At the check-in counter? In the security line? The gate? It doesn't seem possible that I'll ever make it to the gate.

Pilots in their uniforms walk in their particular way toward their flights. I imagine their sunny families in the nice but not so affluent suburbs of Connecticut, New Jersey, and New York. Their sons who collect little model airplanes and show off by knowing all the names — Cessna, Piper Cub, Mooney, 747. I can see my father's TWA captain's uniform and hat hung up on the old-fashioned coatrack in his den and remember how handsome I thought he was when I was young. How he looked like a movie star in those dark pressed pants and crisp white shirts. My father. *How did this happen,* I imagine him asking when he hears about what is about to go down. *How did it come to this, Willie?*

There is little distance between the check-in counter and security. I have no idea what to do or where to go. If they're going to arrest me, why haven't they done it by now? I think of getting back in a cab and heading into the city, but I begin to doubt my perceptions. It must be the drugs, must be paranoia. I'm too small in the grand scheme of things, I reason, to warrant a battalion of JCPenney guys and a hotel stakeout.

I need to ditch the drugs and the pipe. I see a bathroom to the left of the security area and quickly make a beeline there. As I enter, it's empty. Two stalls and three urinals. I go to a stall with the intention of flushing the bag and the pipe, but when I get in and close the door, I see the toilet has only a trickle of water and seems to be running without stop. It won't flush. I check the next one and it's the same. I think maybe they've disabled them so I can't flush my stuff. I feel like a trapped animal. I hear someone enter and quickly pull down my jeans and sit on the toilet. Minutes pass and I barely move. I try not to make a sound at first but then realize that of course he can see my feet and that I should pretend to behave normally. As if I am going to the bathroom. Whoever entered doesn't leave and I begin to imagine there is actually a whole SWAT team of DEA agents and police silently filling the room. It's almost impossible not to peek under the stall to see if there are, as I fear, a sea of boots and shoes. But part of me also wants to prolong not knowing as long as possible. To my left is a toilet paper holder and I slowly tear off some sheets and go through the motions of wiping and the audible pantomime of actually using the toilet. At some point it occurs to me that the only thing I can do is wipe down the pipe and bag for fingerprints, wrap them in toilet paper, and place them under the plastic casing of the dispenser. It crosses my mind to throw the crack in the toilet, let it dissolve in the water and hope the residue disappears eventually; but there is something in me that holds back, that can't bear to watch the drugs erode to nothing. I start imagining the difference in jail sentences—ten years with a bag of crack? probation with just a pipe? Still, I wipe down the pipe and bag, wrap them carefully in toilet paper, and stash it all in the dispenser. I do this as quietly as I can and then pull up my jeans, buckle my belt, and open the door to the stall as if it is the last free second of my life.

Standing against the wall, next to the entrance, is an airport security guard. He looks right at me as I walk to the sink to wash my hands. As I head out past him, he moves from the wall toward the stalls and our arms brush lightly against each other's as I pass into the terminal and away from security, toward the escalator.

I try to keep calm as I descend into the baggage area. There is no doubt in my mind that the security guard has headed straight for the toilet dispenser. I don't look back, but I can feel the eyes of a hundred cops and agents on me as I move past the carousels and up toward another escalator. I wander for twenty minutes or so before making my way back to the security area. I stand next to the stairs going up to the third floor and watch the long line of tourists and businessmen and students waiting to take their belts and shoes off before passing through the metal detectors. I see a man wearing gray slacks, a nylon pullover, and plain shoes. He's one of the JCPenney guys from the hotel lobby who got in the car, and now he's here, several feet away, looking right at me. Just past him, back toward the check-in counter, is an older woman, walking slowly, pulling a suitcase on wheels and talking into a cell phone. I notice the blandness of the suitcase, her shoes, her jacket. It's kindred somehow with his. And then, in the minutes that follow, like seeing one water tower in a city skyline and then suddenly seeing them all, I see dozens of these people. Blandly dressed, middle-aged, suitcase-pulling, cell-phone-clutching zombies whose slow, deliberate movements all appear choreographed in response to mine.

I wander the airport for what seems like hours before getting in the line for security. I occasionally get brazen with some of the people I think are following me, look them squarely in the eye and smile, even joke several times that this must be a tedious assignment. They usually respond with a smirk or a rolled eye. At one point, when the tension is great, I imagine jumping from the third-floor balcony next to the escalator to avoid the arrest I know is coming. But the height looks too meager, not capable of causing more than a broken leg or two.

Later, bone-tired from hours of pacing the airport in a state of sustained panic and crashing from nearly a week of getting high, I finally turn to one of these guys, a younger one, and ask, *Why don't you just get it over with?* to which he chuckles and says, *It's much more fun later, once you're somewhere else. Just wait.* I am certain he says this. I freeze at these words and decide finally to get in line, take my shoes and belt off, and go through the metal detector. It's not possible that I will make it to the other side, and I'm now so wrung out that I just need it to be over.

But I make it through. I make it through and feel, briefly, cautiously, elated. Maybe it's all in my head. Maybe it's just the drugs, whose good effects have all fled, leaving the body that held them shattered and its mind delusional. I make it to the gate and the flight is already boarding. I hesitate a few times as I see, again, a few of the JCPenneys wandering around the seating area near the gate. The words of the younger Penney ring in my head but I am desperate for a vodka and somewhere in my bag are over-the-counter sleeping pills. If I can just crash in that big plush seat and pass out, I will be okay. If I can just get on that plane and away from these goons, I know I will be safe. So I march over to the check-in, hand the ticket agent my boarding pass, and get on.

My seat is on the aisle, in the second row to the right. Never has anything looked so welcoming. I sit down and begin to feel the high panic of the last two and a half hours slowly fade. I exhale and look out the window to the tarmac and ground crew loading luggage. This is the first time I realize that the bag I checked the day before was on a flight I never boarded. Worrying about a lost bag now seems like a lucky luxury and I decide not to think about it until I get to Berlin.

I stow my tote bag under the seat, sit back up, and close my eyes for a few minutes. Finally, I think, safe. And then, when I turn around to find a stewardess, the wind knocks out of me. I see them. The Penneys. One, two, three, four, at least five of them are sitting all throughout the cabin. At just this moment, one of the stewardesses leans down toward one and speaks softly. About me, no doubt. About the arrest about to take place in Amsterdam or Berlin. Or right here. Right now. The entire cabin suddenly seems to me like a set, like some elaborate stage prop created to replicate the first-class cabin of an airplane. The napkins seem to be flimsy fakes, the stewardesses actresses, and the Penneys androids—half human, half robot, emotionless and menacing.

One of the stewardesses is suddenly at my side. She asks, in a tone that sounds mocking and insincere, if I'd like a drink. I'm frightened by the Penneys, but I'm agitated by her. Angry, even. I ask her if the plane is, in fact, actually going to be landing in Amsterdam. She looks confused, but not as confused as I think she should look, so I ask, *Don't you think this is an awfully complicated piece of theater for just one person?* She looks at me for a few seconds, excuses herself, and walks away. Moments later she returns with the captain, who politely asks me to gather my belongings and follow him off the plane. I can barely move. And even though I know this is the long-awaited arrest that's been coming since I got in the car at the hotel, I am relieved when the captain puts his hand on my shoulder and says, *Let's go.* Like a scolded kid, and with everyone in the cabin watching, I grab my bag and follow him off the plane.

But there is no arrest. Instead, the captain explains to me that after 9/11 they need to be cautious and that what I said to the stewardess alarmed her enough that they don't feel comfortable having me on the flight. I notice his jacket, its hokey military mimicry—epaulets, stripes. Like everything on the plane, his uniform—shabby compared to the memory of my father's—looks like a flimsy, slapped-together costume. He asks if I have been drinking, to which I answer yes, that I get nervous before flying and drank some to calm my nerves. How I form these thoughts and words, I have no idea. I apologize for alarming the stewardess and just as I am about to make my way back toward security, a man in a white shirt with a binder filled with papers arrives. He says he is the head of operations for Continental at Newark and instantly apologizes to me for the confusion. He asks the captain to reconsider and it's immediately clear that, for some reason, this guy really wants me on the flight. The captain respectfully declines and begins to get visibly annoyed when the operations guy presses him further. I stay very quiet as this plays out. The operations guy finally gives up and the captain wishes me luck and heads back to the cockpit. I watch him disappear into the jetway and have to suppress the sudden urge to call out to him. I have no idea what I'd say if I did, but I know that when he's gone, I want him to come back.

The operations guy asks to see my passport and continues to be apologetic. I tell him it's fine, that I'll just go home and fly out tomorrow. He tells me not to worry, that he'll have me on another plane tonight. He steps away, makes a few phone calls on his cell, just out of earshot, and comes back to say that he's booked me, first class, on an Air France flight that goes to Berlin through Paris. It's all taken care of, and the flight departs in forty-five minutes from a nearby gate. Another person with binders arrives. The little group escorts me to an Air France counter, where a ticket is produced, and then to the gate. I am there for less than ten minutes when the flight begins to board. At this point things have moved so swiftly that I've barely been able to keep pace. I do, though, have a strong sense that someone — not just the operations guy from Continental — wants me on a flight tonight.

And then I see them. Three Penneys standing near the gate. Glancing my way, holding tickets, huddled together like the Three Stooges of badly dressed espionage. At first, I'm angry. And then the last words of the young Penney from before roar through my head.

Just wait.

The people continue to board the plane over the next fifteen minutes until the waiting area around the gate is nearly empty. A few last-minute stragglers wander over, and several people rush to the ticket agent with their boarding passes, relieved not to have missed the flight. Finally, there are just the three Penneys and me. The ticket agent speaks to them. They remain near the desk but don't board. One of the ticket agents comes up to me and asks if I have a ticket for this flight and tells me that it's the last call for boarding. I tell her I get panic attacks and am not sure I'll be flying tonight. I ask if everyone is on board and she gestures to the Penneys and says there are a few left to get on but the flight is nearly fully boarded. I tell her I need a minute. Again, as before, I feel as if I am at some terribly important juncture. If I go, I might get arrested in Paris or Berlin. If I stay, I might get arrested here. If I go and don't get arrested, all might be fine after a few rough days with Noah. If I stay here and somehow don't get arrested, I will keep using. This I know.

So I stand up, turn away from the gate, and expect to get arrested. I look back once and see two of the Penneys walk over to see if I'm walking back toward security. I don't turn back again and start heading out toward baggage claim. I know that I won't make it to the taxi stand. I'm about to be swarmed with Penneys, police, airport security, and God knows who else. The last lines from a novel I worked with years ago somehow surface through the panic. *It would be now,* they read. *It would be now.*

I fish for my cell phone and see that it's on its last bar, which is blinking red. I call David. It's after eleven and his wife, Susie, picks up. I apologize and tell her it's important and ask if David is there. They are clearly in bed. He picks up, asks what's going on. I tell him I'm about to get arrested for drugs at Newark Airport and that I need him to find a good lawyer. I'm probably shouting when I tell him he has to move fast because he shushes me and tells me to calm down. He asks where I am in the airport and I tell him I'm about to pass out of the departure gate into the baggage claim area. He says to just stay on the line and get in a taxi and come home. I tell him I'm not going to make it to the taxi and then the line goes silent. The battery dies. I keep walking. No one is stopping me. I cross the departure terminal and into baggage claim. Suddenly the Penneys have all disappeared. I'm convinced they've raced out of the terminal through the upper level and are waiting at the taxi stand. I walk out of the baggage claim area, through the automatic doors, and cross the street. A taxi comes up. I get in. The driver asks, *Where to?* I say, *One Fifth Avenue in Manhattan,* but because I expect we'll be pulled over before we leave the airport, I warn him it's going to be a short ride. He grumbles and pulls away from the curb. I look at his ID and the photo is unobstructed and shows the same gray-haired, bearded Indian man driving the cab.

I'm floating in a state of shock. Every second that passes, every inch the taxi moves forward without sirens and the glare of flashing lights seems like a miracle. Then it occurs to me that they're all probably just waiting at the apartment. I ask the driver if I can use his cell phone. He passes it back and I call David. *I'm in the cab*, I tell him, *but I don't know that we'll make it to the building*. He says he'll meet me in the lobby and to calm down. I agree as the taxi speeds toward the tunnel, back into the city. I can't believe I've made it this far. I can picture the spectacle of police cars and unmarked DEA vehicles surrounding One Fifth, lights strobing and tenants' faces lit with appalled interest. I wonder if Trevor, my favorite doorman, is on the desk tonight and what he'll think when I get cuffed and carted off.

But there is no spectacle. Just David, with bed hair, bundled in a coat, waiting in the lobby. He looks exhausted and annoyed and says he's spending the night. In the morning we go to breakfast and he asks which rehab I want him to take me to and despite the grim concern I see on his face I answer, *None*.

We sit in the front window at Marquet, on stools, and the day outside and everyone in it flashes like a taunt. This is a shiny world, I think, for the Davids and the Noahs, for people whose lives I can only see as unblemished and lucky. A place where I've been allowed a visit but cannot stay. A place I've already left.

David walks out of the restaurant and doesn't look back. Whatever his last words are, I don't remember, but they are quick and clear and sad.

Under Control

He's ten. It's dinnertime. He's a little more excited than usual because he has a friend over, Kenny, and his uncle Teddy from San Diego is visiting for a few days. He loves Uncle Teddy. He has a pool, asks lots of questions about school, and is one of the only people who can make his father laugh, lighten him up. His mother makes hamburger gravy—a dish that takes ground beef and stretches it out with canned cream of mushroom soup and onion soup mix and is poured over biscuits or rice or mashed potatoes. Or maybe she's made creamed chicken. Same idea as the hamburger gravy but with a bag of frozen vegetables—peas, carrots, pearl onions. These are the dishes she makes—the ones she learned in Youngstown, Ohio, when there was little money, after her father died, the ones she made as a stewardess living in Queens with four roommates. He loves these dishes; will eat them as if there is never enough and have seconds and thirds. His father calls them slop. Tonight he says he can't believe she wanted to feed shit like this to his brother. When he is home from one of his trips, he usually cooks something else — a piece of fish on the grill, a boiled lobster — which is what he's doing tonight.

The kitchen is crowded. His mother fusses at the stove. His older sister, Kim, is setting the table, and his younger brother, Sean, and younger sister, Lisa, are watching TV in the next room. His father's large crystal tumbler is full of Scotch, and his uncle Teddy holds a bottle of beer.

The boys are taunting the lobsters in the sink, making up names for them and running commentary on their crustaceal movements the way sportscasters would a wrestling match. Kenny names the runt Mama-Pet, their nickname for Kim, and the two of them giggle as the bigger lobsters climb all over it. *Oh noooooo...Mama-Pet!* Kenny turns to Kim, who is doing homework at the dinner table, and says, *Run, Mama-Pet! You're getting crushed. Run! Mama-Pet, run!* The two boys can barely speak they are laughing so hard. It goes on and on until Kim storms off with a slammed book and a bloodcurdling *I hate you two!* They love it and are dizzy with laughter. Uncle Teddy laughs, too, and gently tells them they're terrible, but it's clear he is amused.

Dinner is served and his father is quiet. Teddy is younger, but someone outside the family would probably think he was the patriarch, the eldest of the seven brothers and sisters, the leader. Maybe this is why it feels safe to talk at dinner. Maybe the easy laughter in the kitchen and Teddy's smiling approval gives him just the confidence he needs to open his mouth. And so he does. He tells Teddy about his soccer team. How they travel to nearby towns; how he plays right inside, sometimes center. He tells him about Joe, the heaviest kid in the class, who is also one of the fastest, and how he plays halfback and scores the most goals. His father is quiet through this but gets up a few times to go to the kitchen to refill his drink. Kenny talks about their classmate Dennis, who, he says, doesn't bathe and lives in a house without running water. Dennis has a deformed eyelid, one that folds over half his left eye even when open, and Kenny explains how this was caused by malnutrition when he was a baby. That his family is so poor they couldn't afford to feed him.

His mother says something nice about Dennis's family. Kim tells Kenny to shut up.

The boys keep chattering—about school, Kenny's sisters, who knows what—and Teddy listens to both of them, patiently, and laughs his quick rat-a-tat-tat laugh, which only eggs them both on.

Lisa plays with her food, and Sean is in the high chair.

From a distance it looks like any other family. From a distance, he looks like any other boy. Laughing with his friend. Talking about soccer. Dressed in cords and turtleneck like all the other boys his age. Even if you looked closely, you couldn't see how he is a boy who prays at night not to wake up.

He says something, something now long forgotten, and his father finally speaks up and says, *Oh, yeah, Willie, is that so?* He challenges whatever was said, whether it be about soccer, Dennis, school, the moths flapping madly against the porch lights outside. It doesn't seem so harsh, but he knows his father is just getting started. Still, he feels emboldened by the hour before in the kitchen—Uncle Teddy, Kenny—he feels in league with them and, so, safe. He talks about something else. It doesn't matter what. His father then says something that no one else understands, but he does. *Looks like you've got it all figured out, Willie,* he taunts. *Looks like you're really on top of things.* As his father speaks, he knows he's gone too far and not to say another word. *Have your act together, do you, Willie?* The voice is all Boston, all Scotch. *All your problems under control? Any problems you want to talk about? Or should I? How about that?* By this point no one will be speaking or understanding what's going on. But he understands. And he's praying that his father will stop and that he won't, not this time, finally start spilling what he knows, what he'll always have over him. He wonders if he's told Uncle Teddy, because Teddy's looking at him oddly now. Is it pity or disgust? He can't tell. His face grows hot in the tense air and finally Uncle Teddy starts to talk about Chris, his son, and how he's in a play or on a team or building a tree house.

The dinner winds down, and the awkward patch is ignored and forgotten. His mother asks for help in the kitchen and complains about how her back is acting up again. *Could be a slipped disk,* she says and sighs. His father rolls his eyes, Kim rushes to scrub dishes at the sink, and he and Kenny carry a few bowls into the kitchen and take off upstairs.

At some point before sleep he heads to the bathroom, and it takes longer than usual. His mother knocks once, Kenny a few times; he runs the water, does the dance, makes the mess and cleans it all up. It's done, but when he returns to his room, where Kenny is already asleep, it seems far from over.

Morning

I've been at the Gansevoort Hotel for almost two weeks. There have been other rooms, in other hotels. They are all near One Fifth — SoHo, the West Village, Chelsea — but feel worlds away, in neighborhoods I've never visited. I check in under names from childhood — Kenny Schweter, Michael Lloyd, Adam Grant-West — and explain that I'm in a fight with my girlfriend and am not looking to be found. No one ever blinks. They simply look at my passport, run the debit card, and hand me a key.

I've been at the Gansevoort the longest. I've stayed only a night or two, four tops, at the other places, 60 Thompson, the W, the Maritime, the Washington Square Hotel. These were after Newark, after the nights at Mark's, and after New Canaan, Connecticut, where my friends Lili and Eliza checked me into Silver Hill, a rehab I immediately checked out of. After I scored from the driver who picked me up, he dropped me at a Courtyard Marriott hotel in Norwalk, where I stayed until the drugs ran out — romancing the prospect of dying a few miles down the road from the hospital where I was born.

I've changed rooms a few times at the Gansevoort and am now in a suite that the manager says, because I am staying at least a few weeks, he's giving me for nearly half price. It didn't just occur to him; when I changed rooms, I asked the person at reception what sort of extended-stay discount they could offer.

Every night I hear shouting from the street — *Billy, keep it up. You better enjoy it while you can. You're lucky you've lasted this long, Billy.* There are vans parked along Gansevoort Street with metal boxes on their roofs that I'm convinced are surveillance vehicles. There are bland American sedans everywhere, and each one, I'm sure of it, is driven by a DEA agent or an undercover cop. Still, each night after midnight, I put on my black Arc'teryx jacket and black Parks & Recreation cap and shuffle out through the lobby and up to 14th Street to a cash machine at the corner bodega. The place has two of them, side by side, and only once am I able to run my card and key in the codes and amounts fast enough to get them to dispense more than the $1,000 limit. Usually I have to wait and get no more than five batches of $200. Night after night I do this and then load up on lighters. I wonder how many others like me the people behind the counter have seen. Hundreds? None?

I make my way back to the hotel, carrying whatever drugs and stems I have, because I'm terrified someone will raid the room while I'm gone. Twice I have dropped bags of crack in the lobby. My belt at this point has seven holes in it. It began with four. I've carved out one with a knife and two have come from leather shops that I've passed between hotels and cash machines. Still, my jeans are falling down around my hips.

I'm not alone in the room. Malcolm has been with me for four or five, maybe six, days. He turned up with Happy one night and jumped on board for the ride. He went to Dartmouth, he says. He's black, lives in Harlem, is probably no more than thirty, and is beautiful. Doesn't seem gay and can do enormous amounts of drugs without appearing shaky or anxious.

There is a night when I am convinced the room is about to swarm with cops and we race out of the hotel as if it's on fire. We leave everything there—everything besides the drugs—and check into the W near Union Square. I pace the room like a madman, and Malcolm is patient and keeps fixing me glasses of vodka with ice and lime. He distracts me with stories about being on scholarship at Dartmouth and playing football. He dropped out a year ago but plans to return when he's saved enough money or he can get a better break on tuition. He's getting his real-estate license. When I ask, he says he knows Happy from the neighborhood, and when I remind him that Happy lives in Washington Heights, he says that he used to live there, too. Not much of his story seems to hold up but I don't care. He's gentle and sexy and being by myself right now would be unbearable. Being with him makes all the other nights that came before and the prospect of the ones to come seem unspeakably lonely. During some of those nights, I call numbers for escorts listed in the back pages of the *Village Voice* and *New York* magazine. None ever do drugs with me and most stay just exactly one hour. Their skin and their compassion — most at some point say I should slow down, that I might hurt myself — are never enough, never quite what I had in mind, and when they leave, I'm almost always relieved and disappointed.

The room at the W is small compared with the one at the Gansevoort. It's cramped and the ventilation is worrisome since the smoke we make seems to just linger and not cycle through the vents. I'm terrified a fire alarm will go off as it once did at 60 Thompson. I think about checking into a third hotel, but I'm getting worried about money — there is twenty or so thousand left and I've already gone through more than twice that much — so it's the Gansevoort or here.

We gather up what little we have and leave. Heading back into the Gansevoort is terrifying, and yet, as certain as I am that we are about to be busted, I stomp right back into the elevator, down the hall, and into the room. It's precisely how it was when we left it hours ago. I head straight to the window to see if cop cars have pulled up in front of the building. Nothing. No one but the doorman and a few passersby. Then to the closet and the bathroom to see if anyone is lying in wait to ambush us. All is clear, but it takes a few big hits, half a bottle of vodka, and thrashing on the bed with Malcolm for the panic to fade.

Later, as the sun comes up, Malcolm steps out onto the little balcony. *I'm going to have to split soon,* he says. His cell phone has died and he says that he has to go back to his life. I convince him to stay one more night. We have enough to carry us through to early evening when Happy goes back on call, and I promise to really load up. The day clicks by as it usually does, the routine of sex and drinking and hits and ordering food that we barely eat repeats itself from the day before.

Malcolm's talk of his life out in the world makes me think of mine, and I quietly pray for one of these hits to finish me off. I pack each one thicker than I had before and hold the smoke in my lungs a beat or two longer than it feels like I can. My neck throbs and my arm aches and I wonder when. Again, the lines from that novel. *It would be now.*

Malcolm packs up his things in the morning while I doze. I hear the toilet flush in the bathroom and notice he has nearly emptied the ashtray on the bedside table where I keep the drugs. He has left a few rocks and taken many. I let it go. Not because I don't care, but because I knew he would steal, and the night before, while he was in the shower, I hid two whole bags in my blazer jacket to last me through the day until midnight, when I can get more cash. Our good-byes are brief.

The day grinds on. I try to listen to my messages—something I have avoided for days—but my cell phone produces a text message I've never seen before that seems prophetic: *Memory Filled. New Text Rejected.* The message keeps buzzing into the little screen, making it impossible to listen to voice mail. After a few minutes of trying, I give up. As evening comes on, a nerdy boy from room service brings a plate of nachos that I don't eat. The truth is, I order food to have human contact. He is flirty and talks about NYU, where he is studying political science, the five guys he lives with in Williamsburg. As he speaks I am shamed by the youth of him: the pink skin, the clear eyes, the voice that doesn't get snagged on sarcasm or exhaustion. He steps closer as he talks and I can almost smell the Ivory soap he must have used in that crowded loft in Williamsburg early that morning as he showered for work. He could not be closer now, and I could not feel further away. He is a boy at the beginning of everything, untarnished and lovely in a way he does not yet even know. And I am something else, not a boy, with hands covered in burn scabs and black soot from changing the screens on the crack pipes all night. I had, at first, thought about seducing him, but when he finishes talking, I can only scribble my signature on the bill and shrink away. When he leaves, the voices from outside begin to bark louder than usual. I finally am able to listen to a voice mail from Noah that tells me he loves me and is not angry but terrified I am dead. *Just come home.*

I get high and drink, and when the voices outside get too loud and I'm convinced I see a man in the opposite building with a video camera trained on my room, I do a huge hit and decide to go home. To face the music and rush into Noah's arms. I gather up my drugs and stems and clean the crumbs off the table surfaces and head out the door.

A cab pulls up alongside me as I walk out onto Gansevoort Street. It slows, gently, and I hop in. *Home?* the man with a craggy Eastern European face and matching accent asks with a kind smile. I say yes. The music playing in the cab is Louis Armstrong's "What a Wonderful World" and it is calming and magical. The atmosphere twinkles, as if the cab is enchanted. The panic I felt in the room just minutes ago has disappeared. *You're one of them, aren't you?* I ask, as I have a few times to cabdrivers who seem to know where I am going but who only ever smile in response. I check the driver's photo, which, like all the rest since the airport, is obscured by cardboard or paper. I look into the passenger seat up front and see, as I've now seen at least a dozen times, carefully laid out ziplock bags filled with money — single dollars in one, larger bills in another, and coins in yet another. Like all the cabs with knowing drivers, it is immaculately clean. I ask him who he works for and he chuckles and says he can't say. I press and he just laughs. *But you do work for someone and you're not a cabdriver, right?* He laughs more and says, *You're the first one to see.* I can't believe he's crossed the line and acknowledged that he is not a New York City cabdriver. *I knew it!* I say, relieved that these strange encounters with taxicab drivers have not been drug-induced delusions hatched from my paranoia.

The driver seems kind. When he turns around to speak, his eyes dance with light. He is grandfatherly and appears amused. I press on with more questions. *Why don't they just arrest me?* He answers, because they want to watch me. That they have been observing me for a long time, before my recent craziness even, and that it's only now that I've been able to notice. *Is it good?* I ask, and he says, *Yes, it is good. Someone is taking care of you. You are going to be fine.* I ask him who it is and he says he cannot say. But that I am lucky and, again, not to worry. I ask him if they are listening to me in the hotel and he says yes. I ask him to prove it and he says, *Well, you know, you get very upset sometimes. Very nervous and very upset.* I ask him if they hear and watch me have sex and he laughs and says they do but not to worry, they've seen it all before. We pull up to One Fifth, and as we do I feel calm and strangely blessed. *No fare, right?* I ask and he smiles and waves me away. *Don't be so upset, it will all be okay,* he says as I climb out of the cab in front of the building.

I am overcome with a wave of relief, and as I stand there, two people walk by — they are wearing the shoes, the coats, the ear-pieces, the complete JCPenney outfit — and they smile as if I have finally been let in on some great secret. I can now see that all of them, every last Windbreakered one of them, has been looking out for me the entire time. *They've been protecting me!* I say out loud. This is why I have not been arrested. I look around the street, across Fifth Avenue and up 8th Street and see several people looking my way as they walk at that unmistakable pace, that deliberate and performatively normal gait.

In the lobby, Trevor is at the desk and does not seem alarmed to see me. This is still before Noah notifies the building management to call him if any of the doormen or porters see me and before he has the locks changed. I run past Trevor and he shouts hello. When I enter the apartment, it is empty. It hadn't occurred to me that Noah wouldn't be home. I pour a drink and do a hit in the bathroom and pace the living room for what seems like forever. It is strange to be home after being gone these weeks. Benny, my cat, eyes me warily and disappears into the bedroom. The apartment seems smaller than I remembered, more precious, as if each pillow and book and photograph is part of some meticulously arranged exhibit of The Life Before. I wait, and as I do, I play out the scene that will unfold after he returns. He will want me to hand over all the drugs I have on me and agree to go to rehab. I am desperate to see him. Want to hug him and be hugged by him and somehow blink away the last weeks and resume our lives. But the longer I'm there, the more impossible this seems. I don't know how long I stay that night, but it is too long, or not long enough, and I leave.

On the street outside, a cab pulls up and whisks me back to the hotel without instruction. I look at the driver as we pull up, and he shrugs as if to say, Nice try. He puts his hand over the meter and waves me away and, again, I leave another taxi without paying.

The night passes swiftly and I'm awake for every moment, alone. Not long after midnight, Happy comes and I spend all the cash I can get, $1,000. He doesn't say a word as he hands me the bags and the new stems. Doesn't comment on the increasing orders or the fact that I am making them every day. That he has been coming every night for over three weeks.

I have two liters of vodka delivered at a time with buckets of ice, and I always seem to be running out. I do hit after hit and drink heavily in between. I burn my hands badly from pulling, again and again, too hard on the stems. I shower three or four times. Lather up the shampoo as thick and luxuriously as I can, wash my face with the fancy face soap from the hotel, rinse off and feel clean for a little while.

At some point I am convinced one of my contacts has folded up behind my eyeball. I pull on my lid with one hand while the other scratches and pokes into my eye, trying to feel the difference between the flimsy edge of the contact and the slippery surface of my cornea. After an hour or so of this, my eye is stinging from the assault and the entire area is red and swollen. The stinging has gotten worse, and I'm sure it's because I neglected to wash my hands, which are covered in residue. I take a break to clean them off and instantly see the contact lens stuck to the hot-water knob. I face the mirror and it looks as if someone has poured acid into my eye. The agitation of the last few hours boils over and I yell, loudly and to no one, and storm through the room, throwing pillows, clothes, whatever happens in my way. I throw a water pitcher and it smashes on the dresser. The noise stops me. I instantly worry that I've made too much of a racket and that the management will come. I peek through the peephole and under the door off and on for the next few hours. There will be another shower, another hit, another drink, more shampoo, more soap, more water, more peeking under the door and through the peephole.

Around six in the morning I notice that the sun, east of here, across town, is casting light into the sky above the Hudson. It streaks the palest pink behind the low-rise buildings of the meatpacking district. I hadn't noticed when exactly the fury of the night began to ebb, but it has now vanished. As I step out onto the small balcony off the bedroom and inhale the still, chilly air, I feel relieved, depleted, as if some great thrashing has ended. The closing lines of *Sophie's Choice* sound from some far memory: *This was not judgment day, only morning. Morning: excellent and fair.* I speak the words out loud. I laugh at how the word *morning* sounds now like the most beautiful, consoling word I've ever heard, when it has been what I have dreaded so many times. *Morning!* of all things, excellent and fair.

Birds, hundreds of them, circle above the river. They dive and swoop against the barely lit sky. Are they seagulls? I wonder and immediately dismiss the possibility. But what else would they be? They multiply as the pink light expands and mingles more with the lightening blue. Hundreds become thousands, and the sky is a gorgeous riot of wings. It seems as if some panel of the world has been removed and a glimpse of heaven is being allowed. I wonder, for the first time, if I am still alive.

I hold the rail and see two black sedans circle slowly in front of the hotel, one behind the other. The one in front is just below me, and I can see the driver's hands on the steering wheel. Beyond them I notice there are people walking on the sidewalks. Mostly in pairs, several on their own. They are, of course, dressed in the same slacks and shoes and Windbreakers I have seen since Newark. Their footfalls and movements all seem timed to some very particular choreography of urban surveillance. Like the Penneys last night, they do not seem threatening. The birds above them wheel through the sky, and I step back to watch what seems like a meticulously staged theatrical performance. I remember Newark Airport and all the cabs that have miraculously appeared just when I've needed them. I remember the driver the night before and his words as I got out of his magical cab — *it will all be okay.* As I did standing in front of One Fifth, I think perhaps I've been running from something that has been, all the while, on my side. That maybe, if there is an organized system of observation, it might possibly be designed to protect instead of trap. I flush with the idea that something so elaborate and so stealthy could have at its heart concern, maybe love. For several minutes I lean against the railing and face the gentle morning wind.

Eventually I notice the driver in the car below fiddling with a large white card. He is scribbling something with a black marker. His movements are unbearably slow and with a small white cloth he keeps erasing what he's written only to begin writing again. I go back inside the room and smoke a large hit and pour another vodka. When I return to the balcony he is still scribbling. I can see only his arms and torso and hands. His head and face are obscured by the visor. Finally, he places the card on the dashboard in the front window. It says *BARBER*. Now that he is through with the card, his hands begin to move over a small, shiny black box. His fingers blur from the rapid movements and they maneuver there mysteriously for several long minutes. I am sure he is packing a stem of crack. He then removes a lighter from his blazer pocket and begins sparking it. Again and again but not to light or burn anything, just to spark it. He holds the flame a moment and then begins sparking it again. I'm now leaning as far over the railing of the balcony as I can, certain he is signaling me in some cryptic language that I'm just on the verge of understanding. Suddenly everything depends on my understanding what he is communicating to me. I yell out, *What are you trying to tell me?* but he does not make any indication that he's heard.

After a while, he stops sparking the lighter and carefully removes the white card from the dash. Again, he starts wiping and scribbling. Again, slowly. After a time, he begins, even more slowly than before, to write out another word. Once he's finished, he places the card again on the dash. *TORCHER*, it reads, and my mind reels with the connection between this word and the sparking lighter. *What do you mean?* I yell from the balcony. The driver puts the marker away and carefully folds his hands in his lap. I watch him for a long time and he does not move. One by one and pair by pair, the people strolling outside begin to disappear. Slowly, they round their street corners, or fade away behind buildings and trucks.

The driver is as still as a statue, and it is now almost seven o'clock. I am awake and calm, free of worry or loneliness. My body feels light and relaxed and for once doesn't shake or jitter. I have been up all night but feel well rested. There is still pink in the sky, and I have this great urge to go out into the morning and walk. Unlike following the usual routine of wiping down the counters and getting high and then dressed and undressed, I just throw on my jeans and sweater and shoes and head out.

Both cars are gone from the front of the hotel by the time I leave the building. The streets are empty and I walk down Little West 12th Street toward Washington. I only make it a few blocks before I start getting anxious and the magic air that glowed between the buildings just minutes before vanishes and is replaced with the stench of meat and the low grind of delivery trucks.

I make it up to 14th Street, and as I turn back down toward the hotel, a guy my age in a jogging suit and a trucker hat says hello. He is scruffy and cute and fit and looks like just the right thing to lift the descending gloom. He asks if I've been partying and I say yes, and before you know it he's back in my room, getting high. We take off our shirts and kiss awhile. He isn't there very long when my phone rings. I step away from the bed and after wrestling with several rounds of *Memory Filled, New Text Rejected*, I listen to the message. It's from Malcolm, whom I have completely forgotten about and now hear as I would a long-ago friend from summer camp. He sounds serious and his message begins *Hey, Bill, I really need to tell you something...*

I hang up the phone and never hear the rest of that message because it is at that instant that someone knocks on the door. It is loud and urgent, and when I go to the door and look through the peephole, it's Noah.

Where

Grammar school: Nurse's bathroom. Bathroom is at the end of a hall, away from the nurse's desk, has a locked door. Downside: it's the bathroom the principal uses. Upside: no one is ever in the nurse's office. Not even the nurse.

High school: Nurse's bathroom. Dodgy at lunch. Second choice: boys' room next to French class, on the second floor, in the old building. Almost always empty except in the morning before homeroom.

Home: Best is bathroom next to Dad's den at the end of the house, on the other side of the front living and dining rooms (only when Dad is away). In spring, summer, and fall, during good weather, and when Dad is home: the woods. In winter or bad weather when Dad is home: kids' bathroom upstairs, but hurry.

FRIENDS' HOUSES

Derek's: Basement bathroom.

Jenny's: Behind the horse barn or basement bathroom.

Michael's: Upstairs bathroom between Michael's and Lisa's rooms, above garage. If parents are gone or out in the barns, their bathroom at the far end of the house. If house is full, behind barn.

Adam's: His father's church across the street, downstairs bathroom.

Patrick's: Abandoned bathroom downstairs, in the part of the house that's been under construction for years.

Kenny's: THE TOUGHEST HOUSE. Only two bathrooms, both near where people always are. Choose one and pray it's over quickly.

BEAR IN MIND

1. Try to use first-floor bathrooms (people below can hear you jumping).

2. Place rugs, bath mats, and towels in front of toilet to cushion footfalls.

3. If you have no choice but to use an upstairs bathroom: avoid bathrooms above rooms where people are, use extra towels, bath mats, and rugs.

4. Don't overuse toilet paper when cleaning up. It clogs the toilet.

5. If there is a wall near the toilet, pee with your back to it.

Another Door

His family moves when he is seven. It is the summer between second and third grade and it is to a house at the end of a long driveway, near the end of a long road, and fifteen long minutes from a town in the hills of Connecticut that doesn't have a stoplight. The house takes years to renovate, and his parents add bedrooms and porches and a living room and dining room with the most beautiful wood floors that never get used. Money runs out and the upstairs floors, where the bedrooms are, will never be carpeted or finished with proper flooring. They scatter carpet samples and throw rugs over the plywood to keep from getting splinters. From a low, rambling one-story farmhouse, it becomes a large gray Dutch Colonial, and sits at the top of a hill, *one of Connecticut's tallest,* his father says, and there are forty acres of woods and field.

There is a new landscape of doors—another nurse's bathroom

at school, woods to disappear into, barns to go behind, different friends' houses with various pitfalls and out-of-the-way places for jumping and panic and eventual relief.

His third-grade class is small. Twenty or so in the whole grade, ten or so in his class. He is there only a few months when a new kid shows up, a girl. She is small and blond and birdlike and instantly familiar—like a sister or a little mother. She has immediate authority over him, but it is gentle and hard to notice. He understands that she is finer and wiser but also that she is part of him. From the moment she joins his class, he defers to her, looks up to her, and even when he is ignoring her, he worries over her approval. Katherine.

She reads. She is always reading. She asks him what he thinks about the books they read for school. In fourth grade, a book about an immortal family and a girl who falls in love with one of its members after she stumbles upon him in the woods behind her house, drinking from a spring; in fifth grade, a big, sprawling allegorical series of books about a handful of English children who must battle the rise of evil in the world. Later, too soon, she leaves Brontë and Dickens in his cubbyhole. He devours them and worries about the words he doesn't understand and loves them because she does and often sobs at their endings, because for a while he is away, out of time, somewhere he can't remember himself, and it is a shock, always a sad shock, to come back. She talks about these books, and each time, with each book, she sees more and better and has words that dazzle him to transcribe what she sees. He will steal all those words and use them. To himself, in his reports for school, talking to adults, teachers.

With each word he feels a click into a finer self, one more wrinkle smoothed. Her words have a kind of magic, like the garments that carry storybook characters out of their lives. A dress that changes a chimney-sweeping urchin into a princess, a shoe that returns her to the castle after it's all been taken away. She uses the word *desultory* in the eighth grade, and to this very day he works it into conversation the way a swimming champion casually mentions his medals.

They find out their families moved to their small town from towns very close to each other. They find out that they were born in the same hospital, seven days apart. He was born first but he inhaled vomit into his lungs and remained in the nursery for a week longer, so they imagine there was some kind of connection forged in those early, fragile hours when parents didn't exist, only nurses and other October souls screaming to life.

She agrees to kiss him in the eighth grade. It is the day before his thirteenth birthday, and a group, the same group as always—Kenny, Gwen, Adam, Michael, Jennifer—spend the day at the trampoline behind the health food store. Behind the trampoline are the woods, and a long, dark path where they go to make out. On that day she agrees to kiss him, to go down the path, into the woods. It has been discussed during the week and now it is that day, a Sunday, and they're all there.

She stalls. Or hesitates. Or something. He can never remember. He is frustrated, and he and Kenny and a few others go over to the

Nutmeg Pantry to buy candy and soda. She stays, and he's worried that even when he gets back she'll refuse to go down the path with him. The little gang leaves, they cross the shopping center parking lot and then Route 7. They buy whatever they buy and head back. He's slow to keep up, worried that she's changed her mind or chosen someone else. That he'll be the only one who won't go into the woods that day. Everyone crosses back across Route 7 and he trails behind. He makes it to the other side and then everything goes white.

Later, he remembers an ambulance and the voices of the town comforting him. The feeling of being nowhere—between land and sea, life and death, asleep and awake—everything fuzzy at the edges, and coursing through him a great sense of relief, a feeling of flight. Being pulled out, spirited away. He surfaces only briefly from this nowhere and is disappointed when he wakes the next day, fully conscious, in a hospital room, covered in casts.

People talk. They say he and Kenny were playing chicken with the cars. They pass it along as fact and it reaches his mother, who gets very upset. He doesn't find out about the talk until later, but when he does, he silently agrees with the worst things said, even though he has been told they are not true. He never remembers what happened, but a man from the next town gets arrested for driving with heroin and alcohol in his system. He never finds out what happened to this man.

Katherine comes to the hospital with the others and she brings him books. He reads them — all of them — but which ones, he won't remember, except for the tale of children who pass through a wardrobe into a world of unimpeachable good and terrible evil, of ice queens and lions; he will remember that one always. Like in so many of the other books she gives him, there is a magic door to step through — a gurgling spring with water that enchants a family into immortality, a golden ring that turns an ordinary Hobbit boy into the hope for all good in his world, a wardrobe that allows children to escape an unhappy house — some ordinary everyday object that acts as a portal into a world humming with wonder.

Because he can't move yet on crutches, a bed is set up in what his family calls the Backroom. It is a TV room at the end of a long open space that extends from the kitchen and the dining area. The room is two stories high and has a loft with books and games that one can access by a wooden ladder. The far wall of the Backroom has an enormous window that looks out onto an old maple tree that scrapes against the pane and the side of the house. Beyond that, a lawn. And beyond the lawn, the woods. The bedrooms of the house are up the stairs and away from him, and at night he is very much alone. The tree scratches the window, sounds crack from the woods, and a red light blinks on the smoke detector like some kind of evil bead. He will read more and more during this time. Retreat further into himself and feel, in the small bed at the bottom of the large windowed room, breakable.

Friends come and stay the night, teachers bring homework. His mother plays nurse and is attentive to his casts and the physical therapy he's supposed to do every day. She brings him food and wipes his face, and during the day, when she is around, he feels safe. There is a part of him that wishes this time at home with her would last forever. A month or so later, he returns to school, on crutches, and while he's relieved to be able to move again, he's also a little resentful that his old life has resumed, that no one is fussing over and looking out for him.

But before he gets home, before he leaves the hospital, in fact on the first day he gets there, the nurse brings him a bedpan that he is meant to pee into. He is immobile, cannot get himself to the bathroom, and in a flash sees the broken bones as something good, something lucky. A way to somehow shatter the always pattern of fiddling and jumping and upset and relief. Newly thirteen, and there is a little crack in what has up until now been an immovable door. There is, miraculously, hope. He pees into the bedpan and it feels like he's pissing a thousand shards of glass but his hands don't fly to his penis. While he is in the hospital he is able to pee without touching himself, every time.

A year and a half later, chubby, hairless, too pretty, and often mistaken for a girl, he goes to Australia as an exchange student. Between that time and the time in the hospital, there are many moments of triumph when he stands before a urinal and pees without the old ritual. There are also many setbacks, times when he has to retreat into a stall and wrestle with himself for nearly an hour. It goes on like this until the spell that will forever remain a mystery to him begins to fade. It starts when he is still in Australia, when hair finally arrives under his arms and crotch, when muscles gently bloom under his baby fat and inches happen, height happens. These developments occur so quietly and incrementally that he doesn't notice them until he comes home and is at once aware that the energy around him has changed, that people react to him differently. And as all these prayed-for things appear and happen, his old nemesis quietly slinks away. He returns after six months in Australia and never again, not even once, panics before a toilet.

It will all be forgotten: every locked door, every hour he fretted in bathrooms, every flight into the woods where no one could see. It is not until he is twenty-six years old that he remembers that he ever struggled. And then, when he finally does, he remembers it all.

There will never be any explanation for his childhood affliction. Nothing beyond theories, some commingling of psychology and pediatric diagnosis, but nothing concrete or definitive.

Katherine and he will date and kiss and go out and not go out and avoid each other and have dramatic reunions all through grammar school, high school, college, and after. She will go to Scotland to an illustrious university in an ancient town by the sea and read a trilogy by a great Scottish writer about a girl and her family — about everything — that she will quote from often. She will eventually drop out and drift to Montana. A few years later, he will go to a university in Scotland in an ancient city — this one in the hills and not nearly as illustrious — and read that same trilogy and never in his life stop quoting from it. Boyfriends and a husband of hers will refuse to let her see him. Girlfriends and boyfriends of his will eye her warily. As adults they keep their distance. They write many letters. He reads all the books she ever cared about. He carries her opinions and interpretations around as if they are his until at some point, sometime after Scotland, he begins to find books of his own and to shape, slowly, opinions of his own. He graduates from her and both know it, she long before him.

But before that happens, the summer before he goes away to a small college on the eastern shore of Maryland, they drink a bottle of very expensive wine from one of two cases his mother is holding for a dear friend in a bitter divorce. They eventually finish off both cases and find out years later that it was very expensive indeed. They drink that first exquisite bottle of wine, with a griffin on the label, as they sit on a mountain called Indian. She throws pebbles into his shorts until it is clear that she wants him to take them off. She takes hers off, too, and he does the thing he had not done before but she had. It feels like a miracle that it is happening at all, but that it is with her makes it feel blessed, meant to be, but also something like incest. For years he will think it happened in a field her father owned, one night on the way to a play. But it will be her memory, her story, they agree on.

Uptown

How can he be here? How? I look back through the peephole again
and again, and each time I am hoping that the paranoid fantasy
that Noah is at the other side of the door has vanished and there is
no one in the hall. But each time I look, there he is. And not alone.
A large man in a heavy tan coat is standing behind him. He is talking into a cell phone and I'm sure he's a cop or a DEA agent.

It's okay, just let us in, Noah calls out. *Don't get upset, we're here to
help.*

Jesse, the guy on the bed, tenses up and asks what's going on. I
whisper for him to get dressed as quickly as possible, that it's my
boyfriend. He moves like lightning and is up, fully dressed and
with his coat on in seconds. He heads for the door and I tell him to

wait. Wide-eyed and jumpy, he spits, *Only a second, I'm not sticking around.* As quickly as I can, I grab the ashtray on the nightstand and dump the remaining drugs in a plastic bag and stick it, along with the remaining stem, inside my jacket pocket in the closet. I grab a cloth and sloppily wipe down the crumbs and residue on the nightstand and scan the room for other evidence of what's been going on. Jesse moves toward the door as I grab my sweater and jeans from the floor.

Jesse opens the door, does not look back to say good-bye, and pushes past Noah and the man in the tan coat. I'm sitting on the bed as Noah steps into the room. *Let's go,* he says, without even mentioning the guy who has just fled.

The man in the tan coat is named John, and he tells me he is a former DEA agent, that he's pulled a string and called into *the agency* to find out that there is a file on me. Noah then tells me the police have shown up at One Fifth, asking to question me. That my name came up in a drug bust. Mark? I wonder. Stephen? My heart, which is already beating wildly, begins to pound hard with new dread. I'm getting arrested, I think as I eye John, who looks no different from the Penneys.

How did you find this guy? I ask Noah. I'm convinced he's lied to Noah about who he is and that he does not mean well. Noah says a lawyer recommended him and I ask who. I don't know the name, and the more I look at John, the more I think he's snared Noah in a complicated sting to haul me off to jail.

We have to go, John says. *We have to get you out of here.*

It takes over an hour for me to get ready and it still feels like we're rushing. I ask for privacy and load and smoke two huge hits in the bathroom. I let the stem finally cool and put it in my jacket pocket and load the remaining drugs in the stem so I won't have to pack it later should I be able to peel away and take a hit. The high pushes away some of the immediate dread, and I wash my face and hands and run my fingers through my hair. I put on my turtleneck sweater, realize the bathroom is filled with smoke, and switch on the fan. Noah knocks on the bathroom door and I tell him to hold on. The dread returns as the smoke rises up through the vent. I sit on the toilet and take a deep hit off the stem and pray for a heart attack.

We leave the hotel without checking out and jump into a cab on Gansevoort Street. John tells me I'm lucky I haven't been arrested yet. I look up at the driver and the obscured photo on the panel behind him. Jesus, I think, of course. I explain to Noah that nearly every cab I've taken over the last weeks has had a strip of cardboard or paper over the driver's ID photo. That I suspect the drivers are undercover cops or agents of some kind. I try to explain to him about the cabdrivers and the Penneys and that this John here is one of them and the driver, too, and he doesn't know what he's just done to me by putting me in their hands. *You don't know*, I whisper desperately to him as he pats my hand.

I finger the stem in my pocket and know it's good for at least a few more big hits. I also think it probably holds enough to get charged with Intent to Distribute and immediately start worrying about where I can stash it if it looks like they're taking me to a police station. Then I remember the cabdriver is undercover, and as I watch the city streak by outside the window, I start to shake with panic.

Noah puts his arm around me and says we're going somewhere safe to talk. I ask where and he and John signal each other. They don't seem to know what the next beat is, so I ask if we can get something to eat, and by that I mean, though I do not say it, something to drink. I need alcohol in my system to calm down.

We end up in the Seventies off Third Avenue and find a Chinese restaurant with a basement dining room that is nearly empty. I immediately excuse myself to go to the bathroom and take a hard long pull on the stem. After several moments I think I hear full-blown conversations about when to *haul him in* outside the door. I still keep pulling on the stem. It broils in my hand and I dab the edges with cold water to cool it down.

When I return to the table I ask the waitress for a vodka and she says they only have wine and beer, so I ask for a bottle of cold white. Noah begins to object but John turns to the waitress and says fine. It comes and I drink it down like water. I order food of some kind but when it comes I don't touch it.

John explains that I need to check into a psych ward immediately to avoid arrest. Noah nods as he speaks and I'm not sure what to believe. John goes on to say that there is a psychiatrist whom he knows and works with who has secured a bed in the psych ward at New York–Presbyterian Hospital. With these words an image of white sheets and kind nurses and locked doors flashes behind my eyes, and for the first time since Noah and John showed up at the hotel, I feel relief. I can imagine a long sleep there and drugs to calm me down, and without thinking anymore about it, I agree to see the psychiatrist.

A few blocks away we enter a building that looks like an abandoned elementary school. We walk down wide empty halls before arriving at a door straight out of a forties detective movie — frosted glass, stenciled letters. Again, the sense that John has rigged an elaborate sting operation to arrest me rises up like bile. The wine had calmed my panic but it's now back, and at high volume. A frizzy-haired woman in jeans and paisley top comes to the door and greets John with a wide smile. Undercover cop, I think instantly. She gives my arm a tender squeeze and asks us to follow her. *He's just finishing up with someone now,* she calls over her shoulder as she guides us past a room of empty desks and toward a corner office.

I ask if there is a bathroom and she offers to show me the way before John and Noah can say anything. I walk with her back into the hall and to a door marked *MEN*. It's empty, and as fast as I can, I turn on the water in the sink and jump into a stall. The stem is still crammed with drugs so as soon as I find the lighter I fire up a hit, inhale as much smoke as will fit in my lungs, hold it there for as long as I can, and blow the thick cloud out the open window by the stall. Light comes in from outside and dapples the black-and-white tile floor, and for a moment I forget all the people waiting for me. There's a knock on the bathroom door as it opens, and it's Noah.

Everything okay? he asks, and his face registers the smell of smoke in the room. *Have you been getting high?* he asks, and I say, *No, let's go.* He hugs me and tells me how relieved he is that I'm alive, and I'm tempted to fall into his arms, let him sweep all this mess away, but I suspect he is only pulling me close to pat down my jacket and jeans to find the stem and lighter. I wriggle away from him and head to the hall.

The psychiatrist looks like he's from the eighties. Striped red-and-white shirt, suspenders, big horn-rim glasses, wide-wale cords, yellow socks, and tasseled loafers. His hair is curly, and from the half smile he uses with me, I get the feeling he's done a fair bit of drugs himself. He tells me there's a bed ready at the hospital but that it won't be there for long. He signals Noah and John to leave his office and we sit there for a while without speaking. *You high?* he asks, and I tell him yes. *Good,* he says, *enjoy it while it lasts.* He asks what I do, he talks about the books he likes, and then cuts the meeting short and says, *Take it or leave it.*

I'll leave it, I say as I get up from the chair. John and Noah jump up as I come through the door and ask what went on, and I tell them I'm done with this, that I'm leaving. John tells me that I can expect to be arrested before the day is over. His tone is severe, and at this point he genuinely seems alarmed. I shuffle in place and don't know what to do. I'm panicked but I still have money in my account and think if I can just get a pile of sleeping pills and a gallon of vodka I can probably keep this going a few more days and then end it. I am in the waiting room of a psychiatrist's office surrounded by people most of whom I don't know and I begin to sway from the many nights without sleep, the hit I just took in the bathroom, and the wine from before. My head roars with the talk of cops at the apartment, DEA files, getting arrested. I freeze. I stand there and have no idea what to do. I want to run. I want to collapse. I don't want to be arrested. I want Noah to hold me. I want to get high and wipe all this away. I want to be wiped away.

John finally says, *Why don't you just hang on, let's slow down. I know a guy at the Carlyle Hotel a few blocks away who can secure a safe room for you to rest in and think about what to do. Let's just dial this down a little and get you somewhere safe.* Somewhere safe sounds good, and for the first time all day I trust John, have a new sense that he is who he says he is and that he's just trying to keep me from taking off into the city and getting arrested. I agree.

Within an hour I'm in a large, old-fashioned-looking room at the Carlyle with John's colleague, Brian. Brian is quiet and tall and in his midtwenties. John asks Noah to go rest at home and says we will all convene in the morning. Noah's eyes are worried as he gets up from the bed where he's been sitting. *Call me if you need anything,* he says, and leans in to give me a hug. I squeeze him lightly, with my body held away, careful not to let my jacket pocket, where the stem and lighter are, graze his hands. The second he and John walk out the door I am relieved. I walk over to the phone, call room service, and order a large bottle of Ketel One and a bucket of ice. I am crashing and it's time for vodka. Brian says nothing, just sits in a chair and watches quietly.

The vodka comes right away and I stuff a big water glass with ice and fill it to the brim. I ask Brian if he wants any and he laughs and says, *No, thank you.* I swallow down two drinks swiftly and pour a third. I tell Brian I need to take a shower and he says to go right ahead. I bring the drink into the bathroom, lock the door, and turn the shower on. The bathroom is tiny and there is no switch for a fan. But there is a small square window above the shower and I'm soon in the shower, naked and smoking what I think will be a smallish hit, but it turns out there are two or three big hits still left. I suddenly wish I'd brought the bottle of vodka in with me. I pack hits, blow the smoke out the little window into an airshaft, let the steam rise, and soon I am loose. Brian comes to the door once and asks if I am good and I say, *Just unwinding in the shower.* A few minutes pass and, as in the bathroom at the psychiatrist's office, the panic of the day melts away. I decide to save a hit in the stem for later and begin to towel off. I am humming with good energy by this point and the vodka has balanced out the jittery side of the high. *Fuck it,* I think as I walk out into the room with just the towel cinched low on my hips. I put my coat and jeans next to the bed and bring the vodka and the ice bucket to the nightstand. I fix another drink, find the remote control, and lie down.

Brian, who I now notice is curly-haired and green-eyed and has a heavy five-o'clock shadow that reminds me of Noah, seems unfazed as I flip through the channels and drink. I ask him some questions about his job (mostly fishing professional athletes and celebrities out of hotel rooms and getting them into rehab) and what he did before (cop) and find out he has a girlfriend (nice girl, a nurse) and a small house upstate where he goes on weekends. I scooch the towel a little lower on my hips and ask if he minds if I look at porn. He says, *Be my guest,* and I find the Pay-per-view and hit Play. He sits there for a few minutes, laughs at my ridiculous gestures to seduce him, and says he needs to make a phone call.

As he leaves the room it occurs to me that I can get Happy up here and score a bag or two. I need cash but I don't worry about that part as I dig the cell phone out of my coat and dial Happy's number as fast as I can. He picks up, I say *Three hundred and two stems,* the name of the hotel and address, and for him to call me when he's downstairs. Happy sounds unfazed, and I wonder if he's delivered here before. When I hang up, I begin pacing the room, worrying about Brian coming back. Now or never, I think or say, and quickly get dressed, leave the room, get in the elevator, and step out into the lobby of the hotel. I know I have only a few minutes to score the cash and get back to the room before Brian returns. How I'll make the exchange of money and drugs with Happy I can't yet imagine. As the elevator doors open I panic. I think Brian must be somewhere in the lobby and is sure to see me. I head over into Bemelmans Bar and up a flight of steps into a bathroom. It's empty, and I duck into a stall and quickly light a hit off a pipe that is charred from so much use and finally running thin on drugs. But still I pull a decent hit and decide to smash the glass in a fistful of toilet paper and flush it. I take one more big, oily burnt-tasting hit before I crush the thing under my shoe and throw it in the toilet.

The Carlyle's dark bars and various ante-lobbies are a tricky maze, and I cross and recross the sitting area near a bank of phones several times and can't find the exit. This goes on for a while, and as it does, my panic rises. I finally break out onto Madison Avenue and ask a nicely dressed woman if she knows where an ATM is. I worry she'll think I'm mugging her or that she can tell I'm high, but she casually points to a Chase Bank across the street. I take out $800 and run back into the hotel and up to the room.

Brian is still out when Happy calls, and not knowing any other way, and dreading the prospect of leaving the room again, I tell him to come up but that it's going to have to be fast. A minute later he's in the little foyer—white sweatpants, huge earphones, wordless — and though I called for $300, I ask him if he has six and he says he has four and hands me eight bags and two stems.

The tide of relief that passes over me when the door shuts is almost as powerful as the enormous hit I pack in the shiny, clean new stem. I shove the extra stem and bags into my coat pocket, get undressed, wrap the towel around my waist, hop back on the bed, and fix a new drink. By the time Brian returns I am smoking openly and the porn is flickering on the TV screen. *You scored, didn't you?* he asks, and I nod with a wicked smile on my face. *Do you have any idea how close to being arrested you are?* he asks, and I tell him to please relax. That I have one more night of freedom and I promise to stay put if he kicks back and lays off the talk of psych wards and cops. He agrees and sits in the chair next to the dresser.

I go through two liters of vodka and almost three bags of crack as I lie on that bed and talk to Brian and watch porn. I steer the discussion to his girlfriend, sex, and porn, and, for hours, he will manage to keep it clean on his end without disengaging.

At some point in the early morning he falls asleep. I oh-so-gently get off the bed and into my clothes, pack up my few things — phone, stem, drugs, lighter — and tiptoe out of the room, into the hall, and back to the world.

Idiot Wind

It's a small college on the eastern shore of Maryland, and four of us are renting a house twenty minutes away from campus, on the Chesapeake Bay. It's a blue raised ranch with aluminum siding and a deck in back, and to us it's paradise. Ian is a dark-haired, wild-eyed boarding school hellion from New Orleans; Brooks, my roommate from the dorms, is a Cary Grant type from Maryland—Waspy, strangely old-fashioned, friend to all and enemy to none; and there's Jake, a blue-eyed, curly-haired blond peace monkey who bartends in the summer and plays harmonica and sings in a Baltimore band called The Moonshiners.

There is always a keg on the back porch, and in the fridge piles of lamb chops and choice cuts of beef that we steal from the grocery store in the next town. The stealing begins one afternoon when Ian and I are walking through the meat section. He stops and points to an assortment of wrapped packets of lamb chops and whispers, *Billy, c'mon, unzip the pocket on the back of my coat and drop a couple of those beauties in there.* Ian scrunches his face with urgency, his eyes bulge, he pleads in his particular way, *Jesus, Billy, c'mon, what are you doooin'?* and though I'm sure I am going to get caught, I unzip the coat, grab the meat, and slip it in. The coat is an expensive ski jacket with a wide zippered pocket on the back. It holds the meat vertically, and as Ian walks through the store and we check out, there is no sign that he's carrying our dinner on his back. From that day on we never pay for meat. When we go shopping we take Ian's coat.

I read during the day, when I'm skipping class—Hardy and Fitzgerald mostly that year, *Jude the Obscure* a few times. On the weekends I read in my room, the one at the end of the hall, tucked away from the ruckus of the house. There is no one at school or in the house whom I talk to about what I read. I reread Salinger and Knowles and the books of my adolescence. Some of these copies still have Katherine's scribbles in the margins, and I treat them like museum pieces.

Every once in a while someone has coke or acid but for the most part it's pot-around-the-clock. Ian has a red Graphics bong he cleans and recleans and strokes like a pet. I keep a constant stash in my room and smoke off a short plastic bong and listen to Rickie Lee Jones and Bob Dylan and when I'm not reading just stare at the maroon-and-brown tapestry tacked to the ceiling. We road-trip up and down the eastern seaboard—Philadelphia, Baltimore,

Washington, Roanoke, Boston, New York—to see The Dead, Dylan, Neil Young. Mostly it's me and Ian, and mostly it's Dylan.

Brooks is the only one with a steady girlfriend, Shirley, who goes to school in Virginia. I hook up with two or three different girls on a regular basis—all of whom make Ian's face wrinkle with disgust. *Jesus, Billy, what are you dooooin'?* he'll say at the end of the night when it's clear whom I'll be taking back to my room. Jake has girls in Baltimore or in town who don't go to college. We'll never meet them. Ian will hook up with only one girl that I know of—a girl I have made out with a few times and whom I've told Ian I've fallen for—and it will be in the backseat of a car on a trip back from Boston while Brooks and I are in the front. We'll see the whole thing. I'll be mad and he'll say he was asleep and didn't know she was making the moves on him.

One night Jake withdraws money from an ATM and notices a lucky bank error for a sum that makes it seem like a good idea to buy a fresh keg and have some people over. We do and we drink and it gets late and someone notices that Brooks is not with us. Someone else says he's on campus and we decide to go find him. Ian drives, I ride shotgun, and Jake takes the back. We stop at Newt's, a grim honky-tonk bar that has all sorts of specials to lure college kids. Fifty-cent beers to get them in the door and tipsy so that they'll start buying shots. Which is what we do. Tequila. Ian is always several shots ahead of us, but Jake and I are eager to keep up. After last call, we put up stools and chairs and get more free shots. We are all lit in the same way, have the same streaking comet inside us, and agree that heading over to one of the girls' dormitories is the thing to do. Find Brooks. Drag him home. And so we go. Ian blares "Idiot Wind" in the car and shouts the lyrics, *You're an eeeediot, Babe, It's a wonder that you still know how to breathe.* He rocks back and forth against the steering wheel as he wails, and his black hair and red eyes gleam demonlike in the green glow of the Volkswagen dashboard.

It's at least two by the time we get out of the car. We are roaring drunk from the tequila and there is an unstable voltage humming in each of us. Our breath clouds and shimmers in the freezing cold March air, and we move from the car to the dorm like a three-headed monster hell bent on mischief. We tiptoe through the halls and Ian finds a fire extinguisher to bring along for the journey. He pretends to squirt us and at some point it goes off. Glorious plumes of white cloud billow out of the red canister, which is, in that instant, the most extraordinary thing we've ever seen. Ian points his new weapon in the opposite direction, squeezes the handle, and again, a majestic slow-motion miracle blooms out into the hall. Jake and I need to have one, too, so we race upstairs to find two more. Jake finds one and I somehow don't. They go on to spray each other, the halls, the doors, the floor, a girl who is sleeping. We get split up, but there is a sense that we're still connected by some invisible electric tether and only a shout away.

I enter a common area where someone has left a nearly finished quilt. Blue and red squares of fabric sewn together in a groovy mosaic. It reminds me of my mother, and the quilt she made me out of scraps of fabric in high school. Without thinking I gather it in my arms and book into the hall. It's about now that I hear Ian yelling my name. *Billeeeeee, c'mon, Billeeeee.* Occasionally I hear him bark Jake's name. *Jake. We gotta split. Jake, c'mon.* I head back to the hall. Suddenly we all run into one another, and as we do, I see girls coming out of their rooms, shouting. We race for the exit. Someone — one of us? one of the girls? — pulls the fire alarm and almost immediately we hear a siren. The car is parked up behind the bank, and we run through the side parking lot of the dorms and up through the backyard of someone's house. Ian is in full combat mode and pushes us down behind a hedge and barks in a whisper for us to *Stay the fuck quiet.*

And so we do. Police sirens, fire engines, and the fire alarm sound through the town while blue and red lights streak around us. It's now between three and four in the morning and the campus and the surrounding neighborhood are awake. Lights flicker on in the nearby dorms and houses, people pull curtains aside and lean their heads out to see what is going on. We stay there for at least an hour and finally, when things seem to quiet down, we sneak over to Ian's car and drive back to the house. Brooks is there and has already been called by everyone we know who heard Ian screaming our names.

As we walk up to the front door, Brooks looks at me in horror and says, *What the fuck is that?* I look down and am embarrassed to realize that I have been clutching the nearly finished quilt the whole time. I'm so nervous the cops are going to show up any minute that I stuff it into a black garbage bag and shove it under the empty house next door.

We stay up that night, get high, worry, and wait for the phone call from school, which comes, and a day later we are thrown out. Jake never comes back. Ian and I plan to go to UC Boulder together the following fall. Brooks moves into a house with friends in town and finishes the semester.

That spring I go down to Bedford, New York, a few times to visit Ian. His mother moved there from New Orleans when she divorced Ian's father. I'm landscaping with a friend at home, and he's working in a sporting goods store in White Plains. His mother is often away and his brother Sam is in the eighth grade and generally around. Usually Ian scores coke from a friend in Rye and we smoke pot and throw a Frisbee in the afternoon, and at night do lines, drink good beer, and play caps—a game where two people sit on either side of a room and throw beer caps at empty cups placed between their legs until their thumbs bleed from pressing too hard against the serrated metal edges.

One weekend in Bedford we drink so much Guinness and smoke so much weed that by the time the lines come out I've already vomited. We stay up all of Saturday and most of Sunday night and on Monday I am supposed to meet Miho, my family's former Japanese exchange student, in Manhattan. She's in town for the day, and my mother has asked and I've agreed to take her around.

Monday at noon seems a lifetime away as we blare Dylan and do line after line on the breakfast table in Ian's kitchen. We run out around five o'clock Monday morning, take sleeping pills with a few more beers, and head to bed. I'm in a guest room, and at eight o'clock I wake up and suddenly feel wrong. It takes a minute or two to realize that not only have I peed and shit the bed but vomited all over myself. Ian's mother is coming home that day. My head is stinging, and I panic that Ian will find out. I creep from the bed, take off my soiled underwear and T-shirt, and go to the bathroom to rinse the more substantial mess off. I take a shower and then, sheet by sheet, pillow case by pillow case, dismantle the bed and put my clothes on from the night before, which reek of pot and are covered in beer stains. I flip the now-stained mattress, gather up the soiled underwear, T-shirt, and linens, and tiptoe as gently as possible out into the hall, down the stairs, and into the basement, where for some reason I know there is a washer and dryer. I empty the load that's in the washing machine, put it in a basket, and replace it with the horrible load.

Every button I push, cleaning product I open, and door I shut sounds like a rifle shot, and I'm convinced Ian will rumble down the stairs and bellow his trademark *What are you doooing?* Ian could load that phrase with an empire of disgust and contempt. This is a guy who loved Bob Dylan, thought every other musician was a fraud, couldn't stand the state of Maryland, any fat girl or woman, and most everything else that wasn't from Louisiana. I am his friend, but it generally feels like that fragile status is only one wrong band or shitted bed away from being revoked.

I don't want to make any more noise on the stairs, so I sit down there while the clothes wash and dry. Eventually they dry, and by this time it's nearly eleven. I make the bed, gather my things, and call a taxi. I wake Ian up to say good-bye and he scrunches his face and says, *Jeeeesus, Billy, you look like shit.*

This is the last time I see Ian. He won't get into Boulder. I will, but my father will insist that I go back to Maryland and face the wreckage there, which I do. Brooks and I will be roommates until I graduate, and Jake will go back to Baltimore, where he will—and I suspect still does—bartend and play guitar.

I arrive at Rockefeller Center over an hour late for Miho. My clothes reek and the black Aspen cap on my head—one of Ian's, one I wore nearly every day then—is covered with lint and detritus of all kinds from the night before. There is bile rising up at the back of my throat, and I have already thrown up twice on the train.

Miho looks annoyed and impeccable. She has on a yellow Chanel-like suit, red pumps, and a blouse that is so white I can't face it without squinting. She is nineteen but looks like a seasoned executive or a newscaster well into her thirties. She eyes me warily and asks if I am okay. I tell her, *Sort of,* and ask where she wants to go. I should have known: Saks Fifth Avenue, Tiffany, Cartier, Bergdorf, Bonwit Teller, Gucci. We spend the day in places where the security guards keep a close eye on me. It is one of the longest days of my life, and I pop into several delis along the way for aspirin and water.

The city seems like an animated cartoon that I have entered through some great cosmic accident. The security guards are the only ones who notice me: to all others I'm invisible. The ragged shorts, the Aztec cloth belt, the Snowbird T-shirt, and the Aspen cap (neither are places I'd been) are a uniform for another world altogether and not one I'm even comfortable in. People seem so sure of themselves, so securely in their lives as they march up and down Fifth and Madison avenues. Some don't look that much older than me, but they seem carved from matter and shaped by forces I can't even imagine. I will remember them later, often, and they will seem as the city does: golden, magical, daunting.

I don't return to New York for another three years. This is after college, and I'm with my girlfriend Marie, who is nine years older than I am. She sets up an informational meeting with a friend of hers, a book editor at a publishing company — one of the few I'm aware of because it is the house named on the title pages of the Salinger and Dickinson books I've read and reread. I resist and she insists that I at least explore book publishing, which she seems to think is where I belong. I play along a little with her fantasy, but it's as if I were five or six, talking to the big kids at the town beach about diving off the high dive: fun to pretend, impossible to do.

The meeting is one block from Rockefeller Center. The book editor looks at my résumé — the one Marie helped me put together — and frowns. He points to the assistants on the floor outside his office and lets me know that most of them went to Ivy League schools, some of them for both undergraduate and graduate degrees, and that my academic career and job experience are a far cry from anything that would get me in the door at a publishing house like this one. It is exactly as I feared and I am nauseous with shame. Marie is waiting for me by the ice-skating rink, where they light the big Christmas tree each year, I think. I lie and tell her the editor was encouraging, that he thinks there may be something there down the line, just not now. She says, *See, I told you so,* and I agree.

As we have coffee later that day and run an errand for her mother at Brooks Brothers, I am again aware of the security guards, as I was years before with Miho, and believe they can see what I know and Marie seems blind to: that I don't belong here. That this is a place for a sleeker, smarter, better-educated, and altogether finer grade of person. I get on the train that afternoon in Grand Central, thinking the same thing I thought that hungover day three years ago: This is the last time. And: What if it's not?

Beginnings of the End

His first drink is his father's — Scotch — from the bottle, in the woods, with Kenny. They are twelve. It's fall and the leaves are bright around them and everywhere there is the sweet smell of mulchy decay, of rot. They swipe a bottle from the liquor cabinet and scamper down the logging trail with a pack of his mother's cigarettes and a *Playboy* calendar Kenny has gotten from the pharmacy in the next town over.

It tastes bad but he loves it, loves the strange warmth in his chest and the sting in his throat. He has only three or four swigs but it's enough to make him woozy. Enough to give him a toehold in a blurry, blissful place. A place where he doesn't have to bring himself along. What he also loves is the dark project of it. The sneaking into the woods. The stealthy plans, the covert moves.

The intimacy of an illicit collaboration. They giggle, the way they always do. Kenny stops at one swig, wincing at the taste. They barely smoke a cigarette and they howl at more than ogle the naked calendar girls. They will do this together only a few more times. It is, however, just the beginning of his stealing from his father's liquor cabinet. Instead of the woods, he'll bring it to his room, sip it in his window seat from a red-and-orange-striped thermos, and listen to the crickets outside, Bob Dylan, Cat Stevens, Neil Young. He'll barely hear the racket of the house below. This will go on until he leaves for college.

His first drug is a line of crystal meth when he's fifteen. It happens in a cooler in the little market where he works in high school and, later, on breaks from college. The place stays open until ten and sells things like sandwiches, cereal, cigarettes, and gas. A guy named Max who works there gives it to him. Max is older, a sort of bad boy with a dealer girlfriend, someone he's talked to about drugs and inhaled cases of Reddi-wip with ever since they started working nights together. Max offers to give him a try one night and goes into the cooler to set it up — a short, thin line on a box of mozzarella sticks, with a rolled-up dollar bill — behind cases of eggs and soda and half and half. It stings his nose and at first he feels nothing. But then he gets the jolt, the speedy lift Max talks about, and soon he wants another.

They do this off and on for years. Setting up lines in the cooler, ringing up customers, and sipping beer that he keeps under the deli counter. Sometimes it will be cocaine, sometimes crystal. He never really knows the difference, or cares. It passes the time and gives the job a fizziness and sheen that make it bearable.

Pot comes a little later and then it's always around, until he's thirty or so. He'll smoke it nearly every day in college and off and on in his twenties until one night it will taste funny, make him antsy and queasy, and after this it will hold no appeal.

The first time he smokes crack. He never tells this story. Instead he usually says he tried it at a party, that he was pulled into a bedroom by someone he knew, a couple, a friend, someone he didn't know. It's someone different every time. The phony story always sounds less shameful to him, less weird, more normal, even glamorous. But that's not how it happens.

There is a lawyer from his hometown, let's call him Fitz. He's a big fish in the small pond of that small town. His house is large, old, and, in the eyes of those who care about such things, important. He and his wife are social. They belong to the country club, drive beat-up old Volvos and Mercedes, carry monogrammed Bean tote bags everywhere. Everyone knows Fitz.

One early evening in New York he sees Fitz. Fitz sees him. They are somewhere near the small literary agency where he now works, somewhere in the East Fifties. He'll always think it's in the bookstore in the Citicorp building but he's never sure. He is twenty-five now, maybe twenty-six. Fitz says hello first. He's in his sixties, well over six feet tall, silver-haired and handsome in the way the headmaster of a boarding school is handsome. Fitz wears a striped oxford shirt rolled at the sleeves, and liver spots speckle the skin of his hands and forearms.

Why don't we grab a drink at my place, Fitz suggests. And so they go. Soon, twenty blocks away, they are at Fitz's apartment. Both have vodka — he talks about his kids, this one in the Midwest, that one in Bermuda, and one finishing law school in DC. The apartment is in Murray Hill, a large two-bedroom in an old co-op. It smells faintly of mothballs and is decorated like the office of a college admissions officer. The busy print on the simple couch and chairs is navy and burgundy, the curtains are beige, and the dark wood coffee table, its hinges tarnished brass, is covered with family photographs.

A few drinks in and they're talking about college and sex and booze and drugs, and though it should have been perfectly obvious before, he suddenly realizes that Fitz — despite the important house, the kids, the wife, the tote bags — is hitting on him. He's rubbed his neck a few times on the way to the kitchen to fetch more drinks; has moved from the opposite chair to the couch next to him and squeezed his thigh a few times as they talk.

Fitz is telling him now about how every once in a while he likes to get high. Pot mostly, but occasionally something stronger. Fitz asks him if he's ever free-based and he says, without hesitating, yes. He hasn't, but it's occurred to him. He's wondered about it, imagined what it would be like, but it didn't seem to be something he'd ever encounter. Free-basing meant crack, and crack was the stuff of gritty drug busts written up in the Metro section of the *New York Times* and, he thinks, confined mainly to projects and jails. All through the eighties, when he was in high school, crack made headlines for ruining neighborhoods, driving up crime, being famously addictive. A hideous, monstrous scourge, utterly taboo. Something he has always been drawn to, something he has always wanted to try.

He has known only one person who smoked crack: Jackie DiFiore. He and Jackie grew up in the same town where Fitz lives and works. She was four years older and always getting into trouble. She eventually dropped out of high school and, it was rumored, moved to Albany, New York, to live with a black man and became a crack addict. Jackie's story was the most popular cautionary tale parents in their town used to illustrate What Happens When You Use Drugs.

Many years after the night with Fitz, he will remember Mrs. Parsons, his piano teacher when he was twelve. A heavyset Irishwoman who lived down the road who it seemed had at least eight children. She smoked and drank and gossiped and lived with all those kids in a small green house at the edge of a swamp. It looked like a witch's house and sort of sagged into the hill behind it. One day he showed up for his lesson and it became instantly clear that he hadn't practiced. Again. After he'd fumbled a little over a simple étude, she grabbed his hands and told him to stop. *I can see it now,* she thundered. *You're going to grow up and be a crack addict, just like Jackie DiFiore. No doubt in my mind. You are two peas in a pod.*

Fitz goes into the bedroom and comes back with a small vial of what look like chunky milk-colored crystals. He pulls a clear glass tube from his pocket, something he calls a stem, and packs one end with small wire mesh and then a few small bits of the drug, or crumbs, as he says. Fitz carefully hands him the stem and tells him to put it to his lips as he pulls out a lighter. The glass tube is delicate and his hands are shaky. He's afraid he'll spill the drugs but somehow he does not. Fitz flicks on the lighter and passes the flame close to the end of the stem. He draws slowly as he sees the white substance bubble and pop in the flame. A pearly smoke makes its way down the stem, and he draws harder to bring it toward him. Fitz tells him to go gently and he does. Soon his lungs are full and he holds it the way he would hold pot smoke. He exhales and is immediately coughing. The taste is like medicine, or cleaning fluid, but also a little sweet, like limes. The smoke billows out into the living room, past Fitz, like a great unfurling dragon. As he watches the cloud spread and curl, he feels the high at first as a flutter, then a roar. A surge of new energy pounds through every inch of him, and there is a moment of perfect oblivion where he is aware of nothing and everything. A kind of peace breaks out behind his eyes. It spreads down from his temples into his chest, to his hands and everywhere. It storms through him—kinetic, sexual, euphoric—like a magnificent hurricane raging at the speed of light. It is the warmest, most tender caress he has ever felt and then, as it recedes, the coldest hand. He misses the feeling even before it's left him and not only does he want more, he needs it.

Meanwhile, a silver-haired, handsome man from home has his arm around him, is stroking his leg and telling him he's going to pack another hit, a bigger one, that they can share. This second time he tries as hard as he can to go slow, but Fitz says he's still drawing too hard, that he'll burn the stem. He barely pulls and again his lungs are full. Again he coughs and again, but bigger this time, there is this blast of feeling and not feeling, awareness of nothing and everything, a furious energy that makes him go still. Fitz takes the stem back and, after it cools, packs his own hit. While Fitz inhales, he motions him to come toward his lips and it's clear that he is offering to exhale smoke into his mouth. And he does, and they start kissing.

Nothing before this has been as thrilling. This raging tempest streaking through his system as he kisses a man — the second or third he's kissed — who is older than his father, whom he's seen in the grocery store and library of his tiny town his whole life. They will make out, get naked, and move the whole project of stems and drugs and kissing into the bedroom. It will be a dizzy blur of smoke and skin, and it will be the only time he ever does this drug where doom does not eclipse bliss, where the two aren't immediately at war. Doom will hit when he leaves a few hours later and realizes it's near midnight and that he is in no shape to see Nell, his girlfriend — the person he has lived with for more than two years despite his growing attraction to men.

Before he leaves Fitz's apartment he goes into the bathroom and carefully washes his hands, which have grown sooty and burnt from the hot stem. He washes his face and fixes his hair so it doesn't look like he's been thrashing around for hours. He checks his clothes, brushes off his blazer, makes sure all his shirt buttons are buttoned, his collar is straight, his fly zipped. Behind the locked door, in the tiny bathroom off the entryway, he runs through all of this — swiftly, mechanically — at least a dozen times. It's as if he's on autopilot, or responding to some primal, animal instinct to transform from one state to another. He pulls up his socks, rubs the spots off his shoe, and wipes his brow once more. As he checks his hair and gargles with the mouthwash he finds in the medicine cabinet, Fitz knocks a few times to make sure everything is okay. *Be right out,* he calls as he takes one last look in the mirror.

He hunts for a cab on Lexington and hopes Nell has gone to sleep. He is startled how time has changed shape, how six hours has felt like a few minutes. He worries he's left something behind. He's not sure what exactly — he has his wallet, his keys, his tie bunched in his blazer pocket — but he's sure something is now missing.

This will be just before or just after the night he meets Noah. Certainly it is before he tells Nell he has to leave her, before he's introducing Noah to his mother, who tells him he must not tell

Kim, or anyone else in the family who might tell her, because the news might cause her to lose the twins she's recently become pregnant with. Before he introduces Noah to his boss, his friends, and the writers he works with. It is before Noah is known to his world, but which came first—the night he met Noah, the night with Fitz—will never be clear. It was a time when everything seemed like a beginning.

Family Reunion

Noah is the first thing I see when I step out of the elevator at the Maritime Hotel. Half crouched, on one knee, bearded and shaky, he appears both on the verge of sprinting and holding up his hands to protect himself from attack. And there's something else — as if he's been caught at something, as if somehow *he* is the guilty party. I haven't seen him since the night at the Carlyle three days ago.

I sprint past him toward the lobby's door. He calls and I don't pause.

From somewhere else I hear: *Billy!*

Billy?

No one calls me Billy—no one but my family, friends from college, and people I grew up with—and I hear the name now as if it's shouted across a dinner table from childhood.

Billy!

It's my little sister, Lisa. I don't see her but know it's her voice. She's twenty-five but already has a voice—smoke-choked and sad-shattered—that should have taken another twenty years to earn. It's the kind of voice that to some sounds like a good time.

I scan the lobby as I move toward the main door, and there they are. My father. Kim. Lisa. My family. My family minus my mother and little brother, Sean. I can't believe they're here. My father would have had to come down from the hills of New Hampshire where he lives alone; my sister, Kim, from her husband and twin boys in Maine; Lisa from Boston.

I slow for a moment to make sure that the little man in the bright blue Windbreaker and gray New Balance running shoes, standing in the chic, dimly lit lobby of the Maritime Hotel, is actually my father. He has never once, in the twelve years I've lived in New York, stood on the island of Manhattan. He has never once seen where I've lived or the offices where I've worked. And, until now, he's never met Noah. I wonder if I am hallucinating.

Willie, c'mon, the man stammers in a tight Boston accent.

It's him. Looking like J. D. Salinger hauled out of rural seclusion and dropped into a big-city setting that could not appear less comfortable.

I can't get out of there fast enough. As I reach the door, Lisa grabs at my jacket. I can smell her perfume and cigarette smoke as I shake her off and run toward Ninth Avenue. She follows fast behind, screaming at me to come back. A cab jerks up to the curb. I get in and yell, *Go!* which, thank God, it does. The sun blazes off the chrome and glass of oncoming traffic and I have to squint to see Lisa run into the street, hail a cab that barely stops as she yanks the door open and jumps in.

As I shout to the driver not to let the cab behind us follow, I cringe in shame at how cartoonishly awful the situation has become. Like so many other moments, this one feels lifted from an after-school special or *Bright Lights, Big City.* The cabdriver plays his part — rolls his eyes, drives on. Through the rear window, I can see my family and Noah scatter onto the street. It is midday in the city and the world rushes on around them. I am struck by how small they are, this is. How swiftly these unseen little urban dramas are done and gone. Doors click shut, motors roar, taxis squeal away, people disperse. Through the window, I watch them recede to dots. Light flashes from everything and I can barely see.

In the Clear

After three years in remission, my mother's breast cancer has returned. The literary agency Kate and I have started has been open for a few months and we finally have phone lines. I am determined to have a 212 area code and, against the advice of several friends, pick ATT as our carrier because it is the only one that won't saddle us with a 646 or, worse, 347 prefix. This matters to me. Many delays and snafus follow, and I come to find out that Verizon controls the equipment in Manhattan, and ATT is their client, so the glitch in our line has to be dealt with through Verizon but mediated by an ATT troubleshooter in Florida. These phone calls take hours each day. At several points during the first weeks of doing business on cell phones, it is made clear that we can easily have phone service if we just give up and go with Verizon. I refuse, again and again, and hold out for the 212 area code. I even instruct the printer to go ahead and print all the stationery before it's clear we'll be able to use those beautiful 212 numbers ATT assigned us months ago.

During this time I sell more books than I had expected to; with Kate's help, staff the agency with assistants and a foreign-rights director; show up for lunches with publishers and authors; and talk to my sister and mother several times a day. My mother is going to a breast cancer clinic in Boston, driving three hours each way from Connecticut to see a doctor who has laid out a course of treatment. After a few weeks it is decided that she will have a double-radical mastectomy and, on the same day, reconstructive surgery. It means she will be in the operating room for eight or nine hours, but she won't have to go back under if all goes well.

I have started seeing a therapist. This one is not the first. The first one was five years before, a balding, wiry man near Gramercy Park named Dr. Dave. Dave is the guy I see when I am twenty-five and still living with Nell, when the once faint, unobtrusive recognition of male beauty begins to bully its way into something more urgent. At that point, my sexual history with men amounts to a urinal skirmish in a train station bathroom in college and a few makeout sessions with an oncology resident who lives near my first apartment in New York. I chalk these up to curiosity and push them from my mind. But toward the end of my relationship with Nell, before meeting Noah, I become preoccupied with men — their bodies, their voices, their smell. I begin trying to remember what it was like kissing Ron, the oncologist, and am only able to recall the thrill of stubble against my face and the smell of his clean, pressed shirts. I call a phone line a few times, advertised in *The Village Voice* for men cruising for sex, and when Nell is away I meet up with a few of them. Nothing will be as exciting as I remember those first moments with Ron, but I am still drawn back to that phone line—listening to what I imagine as lonely, desolate men trawling the night for sex. I think if I go to a shrink and talk it through, I can make that need, that new urgency, go away, or at least recede to a place where I won't need to act on it.

Without going into the reasons, I ask my boss and several friends for names of therapists and psychiatrists. I see five or six, two of them twice, and finally decide on Dr. Dave. He's $175 an hour— down from his usual $250 because I don't make much money— and he wants to see me twice a week. It takes three or four sessions of examining my attraction to men before we get to my boyhood friends—Kenny, Adam, Michael—and whether or not I had sexual feelings for them. I don't think so, and he presses for memories of seeing their penises and whether or not they saw mine. At one point I say, matter-of-factly, that no one would have seen my penis. When Dr. Dave reminds me that I described seeing Michael's several times as we fly-fished on the Housatonic River, I say, again matter-of-factly, that I never peed in the river but instead always went to shore and into the woods.

Why? he asks.

I don't know, I answer.

Were you ashamed or embarrassed by your penis? he continues.

No, I don't think so.

Then, why?

Why? he repeats.

And then. There I am. Eleven or twelve. In the woods, behind some tangle of branches, thrashing and jumping and manhandling my dick as if it's on fire and I'm trying to put it out. And with that one memory, all at once a million memories. I don't believe them at first, but there is some physical sensation, some old bodily recognition, then and after, that keeps me from dismissing them as crossed wires in my mind.

Dr. Dave and I spend a year and a half remembering all of it — the nurse's bathroom, the blood-spotted underwear, my father. We spend a lot of time on him. What he said, how he said it, how it made me feel. All that. And then, after I meet Noah and we move in together six months later, I grow weary of reoccupying my boyhood struggles and stop seeing Dr. Dave. One day I just don't go. He leaves a few messages, but I pay his bill and don't return his call. I don't say anything about what I remembered to anyone, and after a while I begin again to wonder if I had made it all up. Eventually it recedes and, for the most part, fades from my thoughts.

Now, three years later, I'm thirty years old, and I have left the job I've been in for seven years, the only job I've had in New York, to start an agency with a friend. I have met Noah by now—on a night when Nell is out of town and I call one of those phone lines. He walks into the entryway of my apartment and without speaking we kiss. We talk all night. He is manly but silly, too, and warm, and I tell him I am a year younger than I am, that I went to Harvard, and that my father grew up on Marlborough Street in Boston. I correct the first two lies before morning but leave the last one untouched. It will be my father, years later, when they meet for the first and last time, who will tell Noah that he grew up in Dedham, Mass., a middle-class bedroom town just outside Boston.

We tell everyone that we met at a birthday party in Brooklyn for a client of mine who is an old schoolmate of Noah's. This is the first secret we keep together.

I drink too much, and I can't keep from dialing dealers and staying out until all hours. I'm a crack addict, I know this, Noah knows this, but to everyone else I am a dependable, decent guy with a promising new company and a great boyfriend. We live in a beautiful apartment that Noah's grandmother paid cash for, and we've filled it with vintage photographs and furniture and expensive Persian rugs. From a distance, it looks like an enviable life. Up close, it's partly what it looks like: I'm in love with Noah, but beyond the drug-related infidelities, I've had two affairs — one with a man and another with a woman. It is my firm belief that he has been faithful to me throughout the relationship. We're proud of the apartment, the things we've carefully arranged there, but we both call it One Fifth instead of home.

It feels as if each week, there is some lunch or some dinner or some phone call that is going to blow my cover, reveal that I am not nearly as bright or well read or business savvy or connected as I think people imagine me to be. My bank account is always empty, and when I look at the ledgers at the agency, I wonder how we will pay our employees, the rent, the phone bill, without Kate writing another check to float us. Noah is covering my expenses at home, but we are keeping a tally so that I will pay him back once the money from commissions starts coming into the agency. I remember the lines from a Merwin poem I used to read to Nell all the time, *I have been a poor man living in a rich man's house,* and cringe each time. I often wish it all felt the way it looked, that I could actually be living the life everyone thinks they see. But it feels like a rigged show, one loose cable away from collapse.

Noah is making trips to L.A. and Memphis to rustle up producers and cast and money for the film he has been working on for years. When he is away, I call Rico or Happy or go see Julio, a guy I meet through another guy I met at Fitz's place on the second and last time I went there. This guy, a twenty-year-old Hispanic kid with gray teeth, will invite me to Julio's, and I will end up going there for years. People come to Julio's and he lets them do drugs and have sex, as long as they share both. These nights were once few and far between — every two or three months — but now they are every other week, and while they would once end around one, they are now creeping closer and closer toward dawn.

After another rough morning, after Noah has begged me to get help, I agree to see a psychiatrist who specializes in addiction issues. We get a name from a college friend of Noah's and I go. His office is in his very large, very elegant Riverside Drive apartment. It's a short meeting. He asks why I'm there. I tell him about my drug use and how I want to stop but can't seem to and he asks about my drinking. *My drinking?* I ask, as if he's suddenly mentioned the weather in Peru or the price of IBM stock. He says I need to stop drinking before he will agree to see me and I politely excuse myself and leave.

Half a year later, after another string of bad nights, there is another name, another therapist, recommended by some other friend. This one is different, calls himself a Harm Reduction Counselor, which is another way of saying someone who helps you plan your alcohol and drug use, to get it under control. I go to this person once. He is a very attractive man in his early forties with a chic apartment-like office in Chelsea. We make an elaborate plan — this number of drinks a night, that number of times I will smoke crack a month — and I'm excited that my drinking and drug use are now doctor approved. Within a week I exceed the limits we've established and then miss the second appointment because of staying up all night the night before. I never return.

Months later: another rough morning, another name from a friend of Noah's. This time it's Gary, and he's gentle and sweet and his office is a few blocks from the agency. Gary asks why I have come to see him and I tell him. He pokes around about the childhood stuff, we talk about the peeing, the hard father, the frightened mother. How they met when he was a pilot for TWA and she was a young, pretty stewardess. When we get to the part about my father, he asks what my mother said at the dinner table when things got rough. I describe how cruel he was to her, how poor she was growing up in Youngstown, how much younger she is than my father, how her own father died when she was a teenager. He says, *Fine fine fine, but what did she say? Where was she?*

Amazing, the power of three words. These will open up such a can of worms. I will sit there and think about all the sessions with Dr. Dave, when I went through, blow by blow, how my father was during that time — how he sounded, what he said — and realize that we never talked about her. Not once. *She was one of us,* I think, and maybe even say. He was awful to her. Criticized her cooking, her clothes, her intelligence, her interests, her friends. Just as he did with me and with Kim and, to a lesser extent, Lisa and Sean. But I can't remember my mother beyond this shared circumstance. Can't remember her saying anything to me about my problem. Acknowledging it, even. Can't remember a word of comfort or concern about any of it. Broken legs, yes. Mean teachers, you bet.

But this, never. Nor can I even see her at those dinner tables when guests were over, when my father would get tipsy and begin his taunting and threatening. It's as if that whole corridor of my growing up held only me and my father, and while it happened in the same rooms, with everyone else, no one else saw or heard what was going on. I suddenly feel very tired.

About six months later my mother calls to say that her mammogram has come back with bad news, that her cancer has returned and she's going to Boston for more tests. I have called her only rarely over the past months. The sessions with Gary are like removing all the photographs of my mother from the family album and replacing them with someone who resembles her but is clearly someone else, someone I am only now beginning to see. She has been confused and hurt by my spare contact, as we used to speak several times a week. She complains to Kim, and Kim asks me what's going on. I tell her it's been incredibly busy at work.

After the call about the bad mammogram, I am in touch more. It takes a few weeks, but the seriousness of what's going on sinks in. Soon she is scheduled for surgery and the doctors tell us that it's a long shot that they'll be able to remove all of the cancer, and, if they do, an even longer shot that it won't return, even after an aggressive course of chemotherapy.

Kim and I go over our mother's finances. There are piles of credit-card bills, and she's still digging out from the mountain of legal fees that came with divorcing my father a few years before. It has been a long and messy divorce, and at one point she asks me to fly up to New Hampshire, where they are living, to testify in court on her behalf—to uphold a restraining order against my father. I fly up, though before I do, the judge says I don't have to, that he will uphold the restraining order without my testimony. I'm relieved but still feel ashamed as I see my father, briefly and without words, in the lobby of the courthouse.

Insurance is covering most of my mother's treatment, but there are ancillary bills adding up and she hasn't been able to paint any of the murals or portraits she's been commissioned to paint, which is how she supports herself; nor will she be able to for a long time after the surgery. We talk seriously about what our roles will need to be, financially, and I pretend I am not worried and that money has begun to flow into the agency. My family thinks of me as a success, and I don't want to tarnish that image. Kim tells me that our mother has decided I should be executor of her will and that papers to that effect will need to be signed. *She may not make it,* Kim says, and the words just hang there.

This is the spring of 2001. My mother's surgery is in May, and I fly to Boston. Kim has been there all week with my little sister, Lisa, who lives nearby. Sean is now nineteen and sullenly haunts the halls and rooms around the hospital. The surgery is successful and when we're allowed to go in and see her, our mother appears half her usual size and weight—withered and weak and swimming in the hospital gown that falls off her shoulders. I have not seen her for months, and as she speaks, her eyes tear and it seems that her words are too difficult to craft and propel into the world. When I go to the hall and call Noah, I break down and start cying, out of control and awkwardly. Everything—the business, the late nights, the worry about money, the feeling of not being able to live this life I've constructed—seems overwhelming, and now suddenly my mother, whom I haven't spoken to for more than a few minutes at a time over the last six months and who looks like she's dying and I've messed it all up and won't be able to make it right. Through the shaky phone line Noah tells me not to worry, that everything will be okay. I eventually stop sobbing, and as we say good-bye it feels as if he is very far away.

We sit in the hospital room with my mother while she sleeps and whisper as the nurses come in and out and fuss with the tubes and charts around her. Her surgeon, a tall, dark-haired man in his forties with a heavy five-o'clock shadow, comes in and tells us that there were complications with the reconstruction and that they may have to go back in in a few days, but the surgery to remove the cancer and the lymph nodes went very well. I think about the fact that this guy stood over my mother all day and had her life in his hands. My job, the agency, and all my worries shrivel next to this superhero and, not for the first time that day, I feel ashamed.

The day in the hospital ticks by, and at some point, there is a rustle at the door and, miraculously, it's Noah, smiling, holding bags filled with food from Dean & Deluca. After our phone call he booked a flight and came as soon as he could. It feels as if the floor of the world that had fallen away when I walked into the hospital has suddenly returned. Noah hugs me and I hang on to him for as long as I can.

My mother will move back to her small new house in Connecticut, the one she bought after her divorce, which sits in a field in a small town next to the small town where I grew up. Her many friends will drive her to her chemo and radiation treatments, back and forth to Boston when she needs to see her doctors there, bring her meals round the clock for months, and feed her dog, and slowly, very slowly, she will transform from the pale, bruised waif we saw in the hospital bed back to her cherubic, healthy self. Her hair will return, thinner than before, but when five years pass and she is, as the doctors say, *in the clear,* you will not be able to tell how close she came to death. She and I will see each other and speak often in the first year of her recovery. My mother blameless and wounded is someone I am comfortable with, and the way we are with each other resembles the way we were when I was an adolescent and even after — attentive, sympathetic, encouraging. But as she gets healthier and returns to her life, I will call less and less, limit my visits to Christmas, and, as before, drift away.

Where

Men's Room at the White Plains Metro-North station (rushed hands, crossing from zipper to zipper at the urinal, and then, quickly, into the stall, a rushed mouth on me until it is suddenly, for the first time with a man, over).

Ron's dorm, three blocks away from my first apartment in New York, twice.

On the phone, in the dark. Nell away. All those voices, all that want.

Apartment high above downtown, after a long night of drinking and dancing and pot, with a writer who is represented by my boss, and his boyfriend. Blurry bodies and a hasty retreat before they wake. The snow falling for the first time that winter.

Steam room at the gym on 57th Street. Middle-aged men. Scared, serious, wedding rings foggy and dull on their fingers.

Bathroom on a Metro-North train. A beautiful young man, older than I am but no more than twenty-five, who had been sitting across the aisle and who motions for me to follow as he walks to the end of the car. Kissing. Just kissing and kind hands palming my face and temples. *It will all be okay,* he whispers as he slides the door open and disappears into another car. How did he know I didn't think it would be?

Love

So, out of order, a memory. It's my fourth night at 60 Thompson.
My fourth night back in the city after checking in and out of Silver
Hill and hiding out in the Courtyard Marriott in Norwalk, Connecticut. I have phoned an escort, let's call him Carlos. Carlos is
dark, Brazilian, in his forties, and he's been here before, once, the
night I checked in. He is quiet, muscular, and a few inches taller
than I am. He costs $400 an hour. I know he has a day job, he's
going to night school for a business degree of some kind, and that
he's from São Paulo. He's on his way. Happy was just here, so I
have plenty of drugs. My phone rings and I can see the number
calling in is Noah's. He must be back from Berlin. Without thinking, and overcome by the sudden need to hear his voice, I pick up.
His tone is gentle, and I end up telling him where I am and that
he can come up, for a little while. I have no idea what will happen, but my need to see him overwhelms my fear of being caught
and dragged home. Within minutes he's at the door. I look at him

through the peephole but his image is warped and, beyond his clothes, he's unrecognizable. I stand on the other side of the door for a while and watch him before I turn the lock. When I let him in, I notice that his beard is heavier than I've ever seen it and he looks thin. I want to run into his arms, but I feel cautious and hold back. He hesitates, too, and we circle each other warily. I've hidden the drugs, my wallet, and my passport in the bathroom under a pile of towels, in case he tries to take them from me. He starts smoking a cigarette and, even in this space, even now, I make a face and say, *Really?* He ignores me and talks about checking out of the hotel, coming with him, going to rehab. I get angry and tell him I will leave the hotel but not go with him. I'll disappear somewhere else, and the next time I won't pick up the phone when he calls. Twenty or so minutes pass and I'm aware of two things: (1) I haven't taken a hit since just before Noah arrived and I need to, and (2) Carlos will be here at any moment. I tell Noah he has to go and that if he doesn't, I will. He says he won't and I begin going through the exaggerated motions of preparing to leave — putting on my shoes, gathering up my jacket — and he tells me to stop. Time is ticking and whatever high I had before has long since passed and I begin to plummet into a jittery funk. I tell Noah he can stay for a few more minutes but that I need to take a hit. He can stay while I do it or he can leave. He says, *Fine, take a hit.* And so I do. I go to the bathroom, close the door, and pull the pipe and bag from under the towels. I load the hit into the stem before leaving the bathroom, and instead of leaving the drugs behind, I stick them in the front pocket of my jeans. I return to the room, sit on the edge of the bed and ask, *You sure you can handle this?* He says he can. I face Noah directly as I light up and draw as much smoke as I can into my lungs. When I exhale I catch his eye, and though

I see how grim his face appears, I can't tell what he's feeling. The high crashing through my system bullies aside his feelings and any normal response I might have to them. I regard him as someone on a departing train would a stranger on a platform. Curious, faintly connected by met gazes, but essentially indifferent. Noah recedes from view and as he does, I tell him about Carlos. I expect him to explode or yell but he stays calm and says, *Fine. I'll stay. If you won't call him and tell him not to show up, I will stay. Don't worry, I'll be fine.* I hear the words as if from across a vast field or a thick pane of glass and say, because it feels this way, *Fine.*

Carlos arrives. He looks at Noah, turns to me, and asks, *Is he staying?* I say, *Yes, for a while.* They eye each other and Carlos sits down on the bed. I smoke a hit. Noah sits in a chair by the draped window. I smoke another. Noah is silent. Carlos motions for me to come sit on the bed and, with pipe and bag and lighter in hand, I do. I pour another vodka and ask him if he'd like anything. He wants a beer, so I grab one from the minibar, open it, and hand it to him. He takes a long pull and takes off his shirt. He is dark and his skin is flawless, and I watch him remove his watch and begin to unlace his shoes. I pack a hit and by the time I exhale I have nearly forgotten about Noah sitting less than three feet from the bed. Carlos and I kiss. He smells like Old Spice and tobacco, a particular mix of smells I associate with my father. We roll around on the bed, and before long I need another hit and a few big swigs of vodka. I load up my stem again and inhale a large hit and turn around toward Noah as I exhale. I try to read his face and don't find anger or disgust or pain. What I see, or at least I think I do, is compassion. As I step to the bar to pour another drink, I ask him if he's had enough and he says,

No, I'm fine. I want to go to him, be with him, and for the first time resent Carlos for being here. I drink and smoke more before returning to the bed and by now my body is alive with desire — roaring, indiscriminate, hungry. Carlos and I are soon completely naked, and when he is on top of me, I turn to Noah and motion to him to come over to the bed. He does and lies down next to me. Carlos and I continue to go at it, and at some point I realize that Noah is holding my hand. I turn to him and his eyes are wet. He caresses my hand and arm and says, *This is okay, you're okay, don't worry, this is okay.* His words, his caressing hand, Carlos on top of me, the drugs and vodka roaring through me — shame, pleasure, care, and approval collide and the worst of the worst no longer seems so bad. One of the most horrible things I can imagine — having sex, high on drugs, in front of Noah — has been reduced to something human, a pain that can be soothed, a monstrous act that can be known and forgiven. *You're okay,* Noah reassures me with his soft voice and gentle strokes, and for a few long moments, I am.

Carlos eventually leaves and Noah and I sit across from each other in chairs by the window. He tells me not to be ashamed of what happened, that I'm not the only one who has messed up in our relationship, that he has, too. He tells me how but I don't believe him. He tells me some of the details but I dismiss them, thinking he's just trying to comfort me.

I tell Noah he has to leave and promise to call him later. He agrees. But I won't call. I'll pack up my things, check out of the hotel, and go to another. I won't remember Noah's visit for a long time. And when I do, every last inch of me will burn with shame. Later still, I will finally be able to look beyond the shame and see how for those few hours, he remained with me, held my hand behind that hotel room door, and told me I was okay. That he loved me. And I will remember how convinced I was that night—as I had been every night with him before—that knowing what he knew, seeing what he'd seen, putting up with what he chose to put up with, he was the only one who ever could. The question I never asked was why.

Blackout

It is the summer of 2003, and through a series of extraordinary miscalculations and mishaps by the power company, New York City has lost electricity. Manhattan is dead and powerless on one of the hottest days of the year. I am walking down lower Fifth Avenue in a sea of bewildered office workers, shoppers, and students. My head is heavy and the late morning sun shines too brightly from the city windows and the chrome of gridlocked cars. I didn't sleep the night before. I was up until dawn smoking crack and came home to find all the lights on in the apartment. Under the mirror, on the bar in the foyer, I find a note scribbled on the back of an envelope: *3:01am, Can't take this.* Noah has recently started checking into hotels when I don't come home. Mostly he ends up at the Sheraton on Park Avenue South.

After a few useless hungover hours at the office, the power quits, the building goes dark, and I leave for home. As I make my way into the crowded street, I think this will be the last day like this. No more nights without sleep, no more Noah checking into hotels. All the gritty details from the night before flash through my mind as they always do. Something about crack, for me at least, will always heighten memory instead of erase it. I will never wake the next morning and forget what I did the night before.

I am barely aware of the mounting crisis of the blackout around me — I'm much more concerned with how to appear rested and loving when I see Noah. As the frantic pedestrians shuffle in herds through the middle of Fifth Avenue, I worry how I will persuade him that this day marks the end of the lost nights, of which there have been too many to count. I believe this. Even though the memory of every morning like this over the last three years — and the memory of believing each one was the last — sits like a toad in the path of my new plan, I still believe, again, that this time will be different. That the old tenacious pattern will be broken.

I know that if the power returns before evening, we'll go to the Knickerbocker. I won't drink. Or I will drink, but only wine. Just one. Or probably two. Talk of the power failure and ensuing chaos will distract us from the horror of the night before. I'll threaten to leave when the conversation drifts to *What can we do about this?* or *You've got to get help.* After a few beats of hard silence we'll talk about the waitress with cancer, how brave she is, how hard she works, how cool the clothes she sews and wears to work are. I'll watch her shoulder through the thick bar crowd with heaping trays of steaks and drinks and wonder if ordering a third glass of wine will provoke Noah into more talk of rehab, outpatient services he's researched, AA. I'll be thinking about just exactly how much I can get away with drinking right now without causing a fuss as the waitress brings us our burgers and fries. This will be the only thing on my mind — *one more* — as she describes the chemotherapy and the exhaustion and the sour stomach and hair loss. *You're amazing,* I'll say as I tap the glass and nod for another, avoiding Noah's glare on the other side of the table. And in a flurry of possibility I'll say, *Actually, make it a vodka.* I won't look his way as I jump up for the bathroom, wondering whether or not he'll be there when I return. When I do, he will be — he always is — and in tears. His pleading for me to stop drinking and get treatment, and my threatening to leave — the restaurant, his life — will continue. Silence will eventually follow, the busy restaurant buzzing around us, a TV star in the corner with her husband, someone from publishing in the next room, several regulars leaning into their cups at the bar. These are our nights at the Knickerbocker. So many nights. But this night, the night of the blackout, will not be one of them.

In the sea of people swarming the streets, suddenly: Noah. He's walking up Fifth Avenue and he sees me just as I see him. I am with my assistant and the rights director from the agency, which is a comfort because I don't want to be alone with him. I don't need to look at his face to know that he's furious. He barely says hello to them and to me he says, *Let's go.* His grandmother is in her apartment on the seventeenth floor of the Sherry Netherland and we need to go to her. *Now.*

I tell him I'll see him there later, and right in front of my colleagues he says, *No way, come with me now.* I say, *Relax,* and he says he will once I come with him. I say good-bye to my colleagues, and instead of making a scene I start walking back up Fifth toward the Sherry. I walk ahead of him nearly the entire way uptown, from 14th Street to 58th. The city is a mess, and because of the fresh memory of 9/11, there is a sense of something bigger than a power failure going on. Rumors of terrorists blowing up power plants ricochet through the streets. The air is thick with calamity.

As we near the Sherry we find a gourmet food store. The fancy kind that caters to the people living north of 57th and south of 60th between Fifth and Madison. They sell wine and even have a machine that chills it instantly that, because a generator has been hooked up, still works. The store is dark save for a few candles, and the owner's wife stands near the locked door and is careful about who she lets in. Noah puts a bottle of Sancerre on the counter, and I grab three more. I do this in front of the shopkeeper intentionally so that Noah can't object. He just shakes his head slowly and when he pulls for his wallet, I hand him four twenties. We load up on things like roast chicken, crackers, and cheese and make our way around the corner to the Sherry.

The building is mainly residential but also has hotel rooms. There are porters and bellhops and managers all over the lobby as we enter and explain that we are there to see Noah's grandmother, or as everyone calls her, Neeny. They recognize us, and one of them escorts us to the stairs that they have lit, on the landings, with candles. Before heading up the stairwell I stop at the lobby mirror to make myself presentable, hide the sleeplessness and hangover. I pat my hair into place, wipe the sweat from my face and brow, tuck in my shirt. Luckily I have some Visine, so I squirt both bloodshot eyes with the stuff and hope that in the dim light Neeny won't be able to see them, or any of me, too clearly.

The stairwell is muggy and hot, and the light flickers against the green-and-gold wallpaper. In this shimmery dark it feels as if we are underwater, moving in slow motion, safe. I am exhausted, but the muffled footfalls and muggy air are calming. We are lugging sacks of wine and groceries in a gilded tunnel with light dancing on our skin. The dread from before starts to fade, and when Noah turns on the landing to see if I am still behind him, his eyes are shining with candle flames and are kind again.

We drink and eat with Neeny, touch each other on the arm affectionately as we animate stories of our vacation in Paris, Noah's movie, and my job. I imagine what Neeny would think if she knew that I had been smoking crack in a project on the Lower East Side the night before, in an apartment with four bolts and a steel bar across the door frame. I imagine her face falling as someone tells her. I drink more Sancerre, glass after glass, and let the tide of wine muffle the exhaustion and the creeping shame. I watch Noah amuse Neeny, flatter her, gently walk her through the dark apartment to her bedroom after dinner, stroking her back as they go. I watch them and love this part of him, this tender part that is so devoted to, and comfortable with, his family.

We sleep on couches in the living room and leave the next morning. We walk home, and all that day restaurants and bodegas and grocery stores are closed. The city grinds to a halt. People look distraught as they confront the locked doors and hastily scribbled *We're Closed* signs all over town. Later that afternoon, the power magically comes back on. Everyone forgets, almost instantly, how helpless they were. Life returns and all is as it was.

We have dinner at the Knickerbocker that night, and it plays out like all the others. Pleas, threats, silences, tears. When I get up to go to the bathroom, I remember the night before; how, after we ate, I stood at Neeny's window, dizzy from Sancerre and lack of sleep, and looked out over the southeast corner of Central Park to the Plaza Hotel, which was dark, darker than all the other buildings. I remember how silent the city was — no low hum of air-conditioning, no stray voices from televisions and radios. And how deserted the Plaza looked, huddled below, humbled. The city around it weary, spent, as if it had finally given up on its striving citizens, lost interest in the bother of it all.

Shelter

Where? the cabdriver asks me as we speed south, away from Chelsea, away from the Maritime, away from my family. Lisa's taxi is nowhere to be seen, and in only a few blocks I'm not thinking about her, about them, anymore. I'm thinking about where to go next. I have half a bag in my pocket and a burnt stem. I need to get somewhere to smoke. We sail past the Gansevoort, where I know I can never return. Not after the morning three days ago with Noah and the private investigator. And not after — I think, but I'm not sure, I can't remember exactly — leaving scrapers and ashtrays caked with drug residue in the room, maybe even a stem. I'm usually hypercareful. Usually I wipe everything down meticulously, repeatedly, so that no one who comes into the room to clean will ever know what has gone on. But we left in such a hurry and I was wild with panic from the stories of the police coming to One Fifth looking for me and DEA investigations. I picture the managers at the Gansevoort and the Maritime combing the rooms with police officers and DEA agents—fingerprinting the vodka glasses and television remote controls, collecting flecks of drugs from the carpet to test in a lab, fishing ATM receipts from the trash cans and calling Chase to get all my details. Nowhere seems safe. Whatever anonymity I enjoyed before now feels like it has disappeared. Noah and the private investigator can find me anywhere. I turn my cell phone off. Didn't Brian say something about how they could track me by my cell phone signal? I'll use pay phones to call Happy. I'll tell him my cell is busted.

I finger the tiny plastic bag in my jeans pocket and trace the shapes of the few medium-size rocks it contains. Where can I go? Where? I need to get somewhere safe, and nowhere is. The cabdriver asks me again where I'm going, and I tell him to go east. East of Fifth, somewhere near Houston. East seems like a frontier. An unexplored country worlds away from the west Village and Chelsea where I have been the last few weeks. As we cross down onto Houston and barrel east, I feel like I am crossing out of a ruined country into a fresh new world. I've been here a million times and yet nothing seems familiar. The buildings, signs, restaurants, and even the people seem generic, implausible, somehow unconvincing as New Yorkers, as New York. Like a film shot in Toronto attempting to mimic Manhattan.

I ask the cabdriver to pull over at Houston and Lafayette. I notice the meter has not been turned on. I also notice that the driver's photo has been covered with a strip of cardboard, but even so, I can make out a name, Singh or something like that, something

Indian or Pakistani. The driver is black and definitely not Indian. I start to panic and fish a ten from my jacket and stick it through the small Plexiglas window. The black, non-Indian, meter-neglecting cabdriver laughs as I scramble out the door.

Where am I going? There is only $9,000 and change in my bank account and the end is in sight. I think through the list of hotels I've been in — Gansevoort, 60 Thompson, Washington Square, W, Maritime. I need someplace new and decide to try the Mercer Hotel. It's the closest and I imagine a clean, serene room with extraordinary soaps and a powerful shower that will wash away the gritty ordeals of the last few days. Maybe this will be the last one.

I walk into the chic, quiet lobby and approach the front desk. I ask a young woman if there is a room and she asks me to wait a moment. She returns a minute or two later with a man, someone in his late thirties or early forties, with glasses. He immediately says, *I'm sorry but there is nothing here for you.* I ask him if there is nothing or if there is just nothing for me. He answers, *I think you heard me,* with a hostile expression. The woman looks embarrassed and will not meet my eye. It takes a few beats for me to fully take in what is happening. It must be clear that I am strung out. I realize I haven't looked at myself in a mirror since leaving my room at the Maritime. Are my eyes bloodshot? Do I smell of smoke and alcohol? I can't remember if I showered this morning. My face prickles with shame and I leave without saying a word.

Out on Mercer Street I'm terrified. I have somehow, without seeing it happen, tripped over some boundary, from the place where one can't tell that I'm a crack addict to the place where it is sufficiently obvious to turn me away. I look at my hands to see if they are shaking. Suddenly, for the first time, I feel as if I might look and act and sound in a way that I am not able to see. Like body odor or bad breath that is only detectable to other people, my movements and my whole bearing could be invisible to me. I try to figure out if people are staring. If they are registering disgust as they walk past. My pants feel very loose. It's been over a week since I've had a new hole punched in my belt, and my navy turtleneck hangs stretched and baggy off my frame and must, it just must, reek. Though I have been doing drugs, drinking liters of vodka a day, not sleeping, and running from hotel to hotel for a month, it dawns on me like a great shock that I might actually look like a junkie. I feel that whatever capacity I'd once had to move through the world undetected has vanished, that *CRACK ADDICT* is written on my forehead in ash, and everyone can see.

I am nowhere and belong nowhere. I can now see how it all happens — the gradual slide down, the arrival at each new unthinkable place — the crack den, the rehab, the jail, the street, the homeless shelter, a quick shock and then a new reality that one adjusts to. Am I now in the purgatory between citizen and nobody, between fine young man and bum?

I start walking. It's late morning and the streets are full. They are full, but somehow it seems that a path is being made for me. As if people are stepping aside, avoiding me. Not wanting to brush up against me. Can they ALL see? Is it THAT obvious? Is there blood on my face? I need to get to a mirror. I see a dingy-looking bar somewhere north of Houston. It's open and I head straight for the bathroom. I lock the door and my hands fly to the bag and stem and lighter and furiously pack a hit. I avoid the mirror, because if there is something hideous there I don't want to see it yet, not before taking a blast. I turn the water on to hide the sound of the lighter. I pack nearly half of what's in the bag into the stem and take a giant hit. I pull what feels like a galaxy of smoke into my lungs and hold it there until I choke for air. The room becomes a billowing white cloud, a sauna of crack smoke, and luckily there is a small window above the sink that I immediately open. Next to the sink is a mirror, and as the thick smoke snakes out through the window, I look. My eyes appear green and red, and the turtleneck collar of my sweater has what looks like white paste on it. The sweater and jacket seem three sizes too big, and there is snot dried and packed below my left nostril. Weeks of beard growth have grown in black, with flecks of silver and blond and red. Silver? I see an old man staring back in the mirror: gaunt, shaky, and frightened. Weathered. I take another hard pull of the stem and blow the smoke out the window. I take another. And another. I sit on the toilet and let the drugs dull the horror of the morning, and a low flame of calm begins to rise. Someone finally knocks. I take another quick hit off the stem before I clean off my sweater and face and splash some water on my cheeks. I look in the mirror again and see that I still look pretty rough. But now it seems slightly funny, less dire. The knock comes again and I pack up my stuff, flush the toilet, and head out through the bar to the street without looking left or right.

I see a cab and wave it down. The name of a newish hotel at Park Avenue South and 26th comes to me — the Giraffe — and I tell the cabdriver to go there. *Kinda far,* he says. Or I think he says. *What did you say?* I ask, and he laughs. I repeat the question and he answers, sarcastically, *Glad to take you anywhere you want to go.* The relief of the hits I've just taken fades quickly as we head up Third Avenue. I start wondering if I should get out of the city, but when I think of places like Florida and Boston, I immediately come up against the problem of finding drugs. Also, I can't travel through an airport in the area, certainly not Newark. I imagine photographs of me posted in all of them, and dozens of Penneys swarming the terminals. The cab slows, caught in traffic. As horns sound around us I feel caged and vulnerable. As if the cab could be surrounded at any moment. I throw a twenty into the driver's seat and get out.

The Giraffe is ten blocks away. I begin to monitor my breath and try to impose a sense of ease as I get closer. *Calm,* I repeat to myself. *Calm.* The hotel is empty and smells like ammonia. Everything is very new and much more corporate than I had imagined. It feels wrong. Still, I go up to a guy at the counter and ask for a room. He's cheerful, in his twenties, and says sure. He asks for my I.D. and starts typing away at his keyboard when an older woman joins him behind the desk and says she'll take over. He looks confused and steps aside as she inspects my passport and the screen he had been typing on. *Oh,* she says, *it looks like we're full up.* The young guy begins to say something but stops himself. *Really?* I ask. *Yes,* she says, *we're booked through the rest of the month.* I start to say something but realize there is nothing to say, so I turn around and head through the door, onto the street, where there are two gridlocked corridors of traffic stalled up and down Park Avenue South. If SoHo had seemed a strange landscape, this bustling, steely sliver of the metropolis is utterly other. There is no soft corner, no shadowy sanctuary to hide in. The cold March sun glares everywhere, shines off the cars in traffic, the glass panes showcasing large restaurants with multiple eating levels, the cuff links and briefcase buckles of the perfectly dressed businessmen marching blankly between appointments. I head back to Third Avenue and then south. Again, it seems as if people are clearing a path for me, stepping aside, making way. I remember a dream I had growing up—about a picnic in the woods and an invisible force that magically lifts all the food off the blankets and carries it beyond the tree line. Everyone—my parents, my sister, childhood friends, our neighbors—accepts that the food is gone, but I refuse to let go of a bag of Cheetos. I'm determined not to lose this bag and as I hold on, thrash alone against the unseen hand pulling just as hard to rip it from me, everyone steps away. One by one, they shrink back to the field's perimeter and refuse to come near me. Walking down Third, I shudder at the spooky precision of what the dream forecast. I feel very small and freakishly large at once. Critical and insignificant. At the very center of things and at the farthest edge.

I remember a building, some kind of subsidized housing development on 23rd Street, where I had once seen what I thought were junkies. The memory flashes through me like a strobe of hope. I remember the place was next to a used-furniture store I had gone to, years before, looking for a rug. I pick up my pace and when I hit 23rd Street, head east toward Second. I see the used-furniture shop and then see the building. I can also see—how can I say this?—my kind, everywhere. Shuffling here and there. Leaning against buildings. Arguing into pay phones. They might as well all be dressed in bright orange jumpsuits, they stand out so clearly to me. I exhale and begin to relax. I lean up against the building and let the sun hit my face. The warmth feels wonderful and it's a relief to stop moving. I feel safe for the first time all day.

After a few minutes, I see a guy who apparently has some kind of authority over the scattered flock outside the building. Someone asks for a light, another pats him on the back. He whistles at a middle-aged woman entering the building. By the way she laughs it's clear they know each other. He has a glint of kindness in his eye, but also a toughness. He squats to smoke a cigarette not too far from where I am standing, and I go over to say hi. We talk for a while. He seems to get me. Get what's up without my saying a word. I feel comfortable. Comfortable enough to ask him if there is a place inside where I can hang out. A place I can duck into and crash and be left alone. *It would be worth someone's while,* I add. As I speak, he half smiles, as if he has been expecting every word. After a pause, he says, *I know just the person. And don't worry, no one will bother you.* He says he'll arrange it and quickly disappears into the building. I go to a cash machine at the bodega next door. Twenty or so minutes later he comes out of the building and says, *It's all set, follow me.* I walk in and we go to a desk. They ask to see my passport, and I am given a sign-in sheet where I write my name and the time. My new friend, whose name I don't know, says to the very old man behind the counter that I'm with him and just visiting.

We go up the elevator to a high floor, fifteen or sixteen, and he asks me if all this has been worth his while. I hand him $200 and he smiles and says, *Yes, well, yes, it has.*

We get off the elevator and head down a hall, and for some reason I've not had a jumpy impulse, a nervous second, since entering the building. Even signing in and showing my passport felt perfectly safe. We stop in front of a door and he knocks gently. I can hear a woman's voice on the other side, something thudding to the ground, and a high, squeaky giggle. The door opens and a small black woman stands there, beaming. *Oh, hello, you're the young man Marshall mentioned. C'mon in.* Her accent is tricky—Cajun, southern, something. She tells me her name is Rosie and to sit right down. My new friend, who I now know is named Marshall, excuses himself. The door clicks behind him, and Rosie and I are suddenly all alone in an apartment the size of three refrigerator boxes. I take a seat on a wicker loveseat heaped on either side with boxes and luggage and bags upon bags spilling with string and Styrofoam and towels. There is a familiar smell in the room. Familiar enough that I ask her if she minds if I get high. She says, in that high voice and tricky little accent, *Why, of course I don't mind, so long as you share.*

As we sit down in Rosie's tiny space, I wonder how Marshall knew what she and I had in common. On the surface we couldn't be a less likely pair, but in one way we are the same. We're the Harold and Maude of crack addicts, I think, as she pulls out a green metal box where she stores her stems, scrapers, and lighters. I pull out my bag and off we go, me and Rosie: cleaning our stems, packing hits, getting high.

My bag is soon empty and I ask her if I could have one of my dealers come up, and she says probably not. If I wanted more, I could give her cash and she would just go get some. She makes it sound so easy, so innocent. As if she were just running to get me some aspirin from the corner deli. And so I give her $400 and she shuffles out of the room. By this time the sun has gone down, and aside from the green Christmas lights Rosie has strung up over her stove, I am sitting in the dark. She is gone an hour or more and after I scrape my stem (and hers) and smoke down the last of the residue, I begin, for the first time since I walked up to this building, to worry about something being wrong. The possibilities begin to hatch in the quiet dark of Rosie's den. Has she stolen from me? I wonder, but then I remember I'm in her apartment. Where would she go? She would eventually have to come back here. Or maybe she's been caught scoring and is being dragged back here with a small army of police officers.

I begin to fear that the whole thing is a setup. That Marshall is an undercover cop or a snitch. How else would someone just conveniently have a sweet little old lady crack addict handy to shelter yours truly from the storm?

But Rosie's no snitch. Rosie's been smoking crack under the Christmas lights and showing me her half-finished art projects. At some point I almost leave but the prospect of a big haul of crack on its way is too powerful to abandon. So I close my eyes and wait.

I'm asleep when Rosie unlocks the door. *Ooh, I'm sorry to take so long. It was a little trouble getting so much. But we did and here I am. I think you'll be pleased.* Who is this angel? I think as I wake up. Rosie lights a candle and asks me to hand her my stem. She gives me another new screen and fusses over the stems and the bags like a chemist and finally passes mine back to me with an enormous rock lodged at the end. *Make up for lost time,* she says, and giggles as I draw in a gale of smoke and think, here, here at Rosie's, this is a place I could die.

Rosie talks about New Orleans. She talks about her mother, who was a painter, and all the famous jazz musicians and artists she knew. Her daughters were talented when they were young but they gave it all up. She isn't going to give up, *ever,* and she gestures around us to all the bags of materials she has collected over the years. *You never know what you'll need,* she says, chuckling, *you never know.* Rosie must weigh only eighty pounds. She is no more than five feet tall and her hair, if she has any, is hidden under a faded silver scarf. All her art projects are half to three-quarters finished. *I'll just glue some beads here and it will be just right. All this needs is an old hairnet to fasten around the edges. One of these days I'll paint the unfinished wood on this one.* None of them look like anything, and they are all just one or two little tasks away from being beautiful. Rosie's hands shake violently as she holds each little almost-beautiful nothing up to the light.

After a few hours of smoking and listening (Rosie never asks any questions), I get restless. The room is too small. Rosie never quiets. And I have a little mountain of drugs in my pocket that makes the world seem manageable.

I leave Rosie a few rocks and a hundred dollars, and she pats my forehead as I go and says, *Come back. Don't forget Rosie. Come back.*

I head out through the brightly lit hallway and down the elevator and sign out at the counter. Humming with drugs and shaky from not eating all day, I'm conscious of how ruined I must appear now. Even worse than this morning.

How will I ever be able to check into a hotel in this state, I wonder, as I walk, as slowly and calmly as I can, out onto 23rd Street. It's late in the evening now. People are out, rushing home from dinner, heading to their softly lit apartments, and feeding their cats or dogs or paying their babysitters. Buses squeal down 23rd Street, and guys from karate practice walk together with their uniforms still on and their workout bags slung over their shoulders. My heart pounds hard behind my chest and blood streaks through my veins like electricity. I feel as light as a wafer and my pants won't stay up. I can't use my phone because I'm afraid I'll be tracked down again. There is just over $8,000 left in my account, and I can't fly anywhere, stay anywhere, appear anywhere I am known. I can't just walk into any hotel, because two have already refused me and that was earlier in the day, several bags of crack ago, when I was more presentable. On the corner of 23rd Street and Second Avenue, I am frozen. Where do I go? Every direction is wrong. *Where?*

Just Here

Noah and I are heading out the door for a few weeks of vacation in Cambridge, Mass. I call my friend Robert, whose lymphoma has recently gone into remission, to check in, see how he's doing. He sounds great. His voice is a cross between Truman Capote's and Charles Nelson Reilly's. He is one of the first editors in publishing who called me when I was a young agent and asked me to lunch. He's in his forties, clearly gay, very smart, and wickedly funny. After that lunch we spoke a few times a week about work, authors we had in common, publishing gossip. Robert's references — professional and literary — often went over my head and I would pretend to understand. If he knew, which I'm sure he did, he never let on.

Robert tells me on the phone that he has to head back into the hospital for something having to do with his lungs. *No big deal,* he says, *not to worry*. I startle for a moment and when I ask him again, he reassures me that it's nothing, that it's routine.

We go up to Cambridge. Noah and I read, go to movies at the Brattle, drink lots of coffee, and walk around and look at Harvard and the great houses spread out on all sides of the campus. What we always do. And then one morning one of Robert's colleagues calls to say that he is dead, that he went into the hospital and it turned out he had pneumonia.

I've known Robert for four or five years, see him every two or three months, and we speak on the phone regularly, but I can't say we are close. He is a part of my work life, and a consistently bright part. His battle with lymphoma has gone on, as far as I know, for a few years. He has been, with me anyway, always vague about the details. His treatment had gotten rough for a while, he left work for several months, but the remission seemed strong. He flew to Europe to go to the opera and dove back into publishing. He was back to normal.

I hang up the phone and after a few stunned, still moments, I start sobbing. I cry for days and can't stop. At dinner, during walks around Cambridge, in the shower, at the gym. I cry uncontrollably. The last time I can remember crying was at the hospital with my mother three or four months before. Eventually the tears stop, but the hard fact of never seeing or hearing Robert again plunks down somewhere in my chest and does not leave.

We come back to New York over Labor Day weekend. There is a memorial service for Robert scheduled on September 10 at the University Club. A writer I represent flies to New York from Chicago on the ninth. Robert edited and adored his novel, which is just about to be published. We go to the memorial service and listen to the writers Robert edited tell stories of how brilliantly he edited their work. How well he took care of them. How much fun he was. Their words make me feel alone, lonely. We go to L'acajou and I start drinking right away. Glass after glass, I drink it like water, and my face prickles with the heat of too much alcohol in my blood. I excuse myself to go to the bathroom and call Julio and tell him to call his dealer, that I'm coming over, with cash. Later, after paying the bill, I say my good-byes, get in a cab, run into Julio's building, and pace the elevator as it crawls to his floor.

That night will go by in a flash. I make it home sometime before eight, but after Noah has left for the day. There is no note on the bar. I have a vague memory of a foreign publisher — German? Dutch? I don't remember — who is scheduled to come into the office. I shower and dress and walk up Fifth Avenue to the office, and my head pounds from all the vodka the night before, and the sky is the most extraordinary cloudless blue I have ever seen. North of 14th Street, I see a young editor I know run across Fifth Avenue in a bright white shirt. I wonder why he's running so fast.

When I walk into the agency, everyone is there. A friend calls just then and says that the Twin Towers have been attacked. Almost immediately the office, the people from the other offices on our

floor, people calling, are hysterical, and there is an image on CNN
.com of one of the towers billowing with smoke. Rumors escalate
and the atmosphere is chaotic and frightened. Noah calls. He is
crying. He asks if I am okay, does not mention the night before,
and says that he is watching the towers from his office window in
SoHo. We arrange to meet at the apartment later.

I suddenly remember that the appointment I have is to get my
hair cut by Seth. I call to see if he is open. He says to come over.
My hair is shaggy, and with my bloodshot eyes and pasty skin,
I think it's more obvious than usual that I've been out all night.
Getting my hair shampooed and cut can't hurt, I think, as I grab
my wallet and head out the door. My assistant asks me where I
am going, and when I tell her, *To get my hair cut,* she stares at me,
speechless.

As I walk west across 25th Street, a jet flies low enough that the
buildings all around me rumble and I crouch on the sidewalk and
cover my head with my arms. It will be the only moment of that
day that won't feel numb. The rest will be surreal and far away, as
if I am watching them on a screen or through a thick lens.

Both towers are still standing when I reach Sixth Avenue. I linger there for a second or two before heading across 22nd Street
to Seth's. Everywhere people are quiet. Everywhere people move
gently, slowly. They are careful with one another.

Seth's place is empty and we listen to the radio as he washes my hair and slowly cuts it. I wonder if he can tell how polluted I am, how strung out from the night before. Unlike when we engage in our usual chatter of gossip, we barely talk and are silent as the report of the first tower falling comes over the radio. Seth's phone rings but he lets it go on and on until the machine picks up. It takes over an hour for him to cut my hair, and I think it is because he doesn't want to be alone. I am grateful to be here, in this seat, safe.

I leave Seth's and walk back to Sixth Avenue, where a throng of people on the corner are all looking south. Something feels off balance and I have a brief flash of vertigo as I follow their gazes downtown to the now bland tumble of buildings there. The towers have fallen. An hour ago they stood there, on fire, billowing with smoke, and now they are gone. *They were just here,* someone says as I try to locate where exactly in the skyline they used to rise from. But in the cloud of soot and smoke that hangs above the blur of buildings that could be any city now, I can't remember where they once were, what it all looked like. I have already forgotten.

Where

When Noah is away: Home.

When Noah is home: Mark's or Julio's or any satellite thereof. Hotels.

If between home and elsewhere: Back of cabs; bathroom in the lobby of One Fifth; stairwell landing between fifth and sixth floors of One Fifth; video booth at porn store on 14th between Sixth and Seventh and the one at 44th and Eighth, near Orso; bathroom at L'acajou; bathroom at LensCrafters on Fifth Avenue; bathroom at McDonald's on Seventh below 14th Street; desk at my office; bathroom at my office; stairwell of office building; in Central Park behind trees and in bathroom stall by Delacorte Theatre;

Westside Highway under shrubs; in basements of buildings under construction, behind Dumpsters, in Dumpsters, anywhere.

In London: Charlotte Street Hotel, back of hired cars (not black cabs), behind hedges at the top of Highbury Fields.

In Paris: On bench in the Place des Vosges, on bed in brothel; in back of a cab driven by guy who gives you a free bag of hash; in stairwell of apartment building; café bathrooms.

BEAR IN MIND

In transit, let stem cool before shoving it in pocket or it will burn through your pants.

The Jesus Year

This is the year of the most nights out. The most notes left on the bar, the most shattered mornings, the most broken promises to drink only two vodkas at dinner, the most abandoned resolutions to stop calling Rico and Happy and Mark and Julio and anyone else who can lead me to getting high, the most calls to my assistant to say I am sick, the most lies.

It's more than three years after my mother's surgery, a year after she stops chemo, and the year Noah makes his movie in Memphis. The agency is doing well. We're turning a profit, and a number of books that I am selling are not only the subject of heated bidding wars among book publishers but go on to be excerpted in places like *The New Yorker* and reviewed well everywhere, and in one case on the cover of the *New York Times Book Review*. And there will be one, a cherished one, that appears like a winking miracle of enchanted audacity which becomes a finalist for the National Book Award.

Before the nomination, before the publication, there will be a lunch given at La Grenouille, a French restaurant in the East 50s. I ask an acquaintance, an almost-friend, Jean, to come. Jean who never goes to lunch. Jean whom I met in the lobby of the Frankfurter Hof hotel when I was twenty-five and who, for years after, invited me to book parties and other gatherings at her terraced penthouse overlooking the East River. Jean's parties always have a funny mix of staggering accomplishment, fame, wealth, political passion, and genuine strangeness. Sometimes there are small dinners and sometimes seats at benefit tables. But as years pass, there is always a seat at the table. And every time feels like the last. The one where I will say the thing that will correct whatever mistaken illusion she has of me and reveal the fraudulent imbecile that I am.

So I invite Jean to the lunch at La Grenouille. I invite her because the book she wrote about the gritty-fabulous rise and fall of a Wasp princess is a favorite of the author of the Winking Miracle. I invite her because of her literary glamour, because she matters to the author, and because she is also a friend of the author's Legendary Editor. For all these reasons, and because she has invited me to so much, and because when she is around I feel, strange and unlikely as it seems, loved, I ask her to come. Impossibly, she agrees, and I am excited for the rare energy she will bring to the event, the likes of which are organized purely to generate energy to launch whatever new literary rocket into orbit. Months go into getting this lunch together. There is a generous friend of the author's who has agreed to sponsor it, and because of the elegance of the restaurant and the influence of the author's Legendary Editor, and the hustling on everyone's part, there is an unusually august group of literary lights scheduled to attend.

Why do certain things shimmer on the horizon with fairy dust and others not? This lunch, on the calendar for months, sparkles in blue ink every time I open that page to pencil something else in on either side. I flush with excitement when anything associated with it crosses my mind or my desk—the book, Jean, La Grenouille, the Legendary Editor—all of it, folded together into a shiny promise of something blessed.

I need a suit, and in a burst of recklessness I go to Saks and pick out a slim black/navy lightly striped Gucci suit that costs over $3,000. The most money I've ever spent on any one piece of clothing. In it, in the dressing room, I look for a moment like someone I don't recognize. Someone who has dozens of suits, dozens of pairs of shoes to go with them, and money to afford them all. Not recognizing yourself in the mirror is like seeing a photo that someone takes of you at a party and having your jealous eye drawn to the unfettered, attractive, someone-who-belongs-everywhere person gazing through the photograph over an impassable distance between their world and yours; you see that lucky bastard who you imagine has never had an uncomfortable, insecure, unadored moment in his life and you despise his ease instantly. And then you find out it's you. It can't be, you're sure it's not you. But when you see that he has your clothes on and, yes, Jesus, yes, he has the same large ear that sticks out and the other, smaller one that lies flat to his head; when you see that it's you, you think for a second: Is it possible that someone might make the same mistaken assumptions about the you who is not you? It shakes you for a moment and you decide that in some essential way, the person staring back through the photograph is actually someone else. Or rather, he doesn't exist. The angle of the photograph and the lie it achieves are like the suit. So if you're standing in a dressing room, looking in the mirror, and see someone who looks like the person in that photograph, you buy the suit, because if that person can't actually exist, it might as well look as if he does.

Two nights before the lunch, I'm at a dinner. I can't remember which one or with whom but a few things can be counted on. I'm at l'acajou. I drink vodka. The waiters and waitresses top off my glass through the night. A gentle calm spreads into my chest with each glass and, gradually, the symphony of usual worries dies down. As those instruments still, and after the brief patch of ease begins to ebb, other sounds rise up from the pit. Agitated strings. Bullying horns. The pesky, restless want that feels like need. As I talk and listen and eat and laugh, I am waving my conducting wand, commanding the instruments to quiet. But as I wave more, I drink more, and as I drink, the sounds rise, become more insistent, and I excuse myself and go to the bathroom and call a number. This time it's Mark's and I arrange to go to his place after dinner. I worry a moment that the lunch for the author of the Winking Miracle is two days away and I need to be in top shape for that. But it's two whole days, I reason. Even if I stay up most of the night, I'll still have a full twenty-four hours to regain my footing.

✦

I go to Mark's and there is a blur of smoke and flesh and other people, and in the morning, this time, I don't want it to end. The lunch is the next day, but still, somehow, it feels far away. A whole day and night and morning between now and then. It will work out. It always does. But this is the first night that wants to be two. Why this one and not the others? I look at the calendar from that time and it is graffitied with ink. Scribbled notes about lunch meetings, coffee dates, phone dates, drinks dates, trips to London, L.A., Frankfurt. Weddings, birthdays, benefits, plays, operas, book parties, screenings. So much to show up for, so much to camouflage for, to worry over. There is no busier period than that year when I am thirty-two and thirty-three. The sunstruck runup to the Jesus year. Someone—was it Marie?—always joked about thirty-three being the Jesus year—how it marked the end of one life and the beginning of another, the end of youth and the beginning of the undebatable status of adulthood. But I was twenty-four when she turned thirty-three, and adulthood seemed a world away.

Why was that the night that became three? Why did all the things that to anyone else, even to me, looked lucky, enviable, feel like burdens? It was the year I got tired, the year I began to give up. It was when the conducting wand broke and the sounds from the pit overwhelmed the conductor and drowned the hall.

I leave Mark's by midday and check into a small hotel around the corner from the agency. It's a cheap tourist hotel, one step up from a hostel, and I go there because Mark's place is too sloppy, too smoke-charred, too exposed. The jittery paranoia I have seen in most of the crack smokers I have known has, during the last three or four times getting high, started to afflict me. This time it's the most nagging, most persistent, and when I am at Mark's, I find myself at the window, seeing what I think are unmarked police cars parked in front of his building. By morning I need to get out of there. I have Rico's number, and I am pretty sure I can get him to deliver more in the afternoon. And so he does, and I stay up all night, alone and with reruns of the dingy and dated cable-access *Robin Byrd Show*, where rough-around-the-edges go-go boys and girls strip and let Robin perform oral sex on them. When this is over, I leave the station on all night. It runs low-tech ads for 1-900 numbers, with naked and half-naked men and women wooing the camera with talk of raunchy phone sex. The hotel room looks out onto an alley, and I lean out and look up at the panels of light reflected from other hotel rooms. Occasionally there will be a silhouette of a man or woman flickering across the brick, and I imagine a million scenarios. Sometimes a sound—a low crack, a muffled scraping, a window slamming shut—will echo through the alley, and a few times I call out, *Hello.*

Morning comes on fast, and by ten o'clock I realize I need to get home to fetch my suit for the lunch at La Grenouille. Noah has left dozens of messages, and beyond one phone call two nights before, saying I was alive and fine and not to worry, I have not called him. I still have a large bag from the night before and it gives me some comfort as I begin to face the day ahead. I reserve the hotel room again and take a cab to One Fifth to get my suit. Thankfully, Noah is not there, so I grab the suit, black shoes, and socks and haul out of the apartment, back into a cab and to the hotel room. It is noon by now and the lunch is at one. I can't believe I've disappeared for two nights and a full day. Noah must be out of his mind with worry. But as much as I know this, I don't call him, don't track him down to let him know I am okay. I left a message on the voice mail for my assistant at eight a.m. to say that I would be going straight to the lunch, so that base is, for now, covered. But the lunch! Oh, Jesus, how can I go in this shape? I sit on the bed, pack the burnt, oily stem from the night before with a large rock, and inhale. My terror over the lunch, Noah, my office, and everything else vanishes like a flame suddenly cut off from oxygen. I roll up in the bedspread and let the flash of warm lightning race through my system. I lie on the bed for what seems like only a few minutes, but when I sit up again, it is five after one. The lunch. The glittering happy event that has sung its siren call for months has already begun, and I am strung out, unshowered, unshaven, and skinny from not eating. I take another hit and rush into the shower. It is almost two by the time I get out of the hotel and into a cab. After a shave and shower and the suit, I look in the mirror and, God help me, I convince myself that I look good. A little gaunt and shaky, but the suit, not to mention the bag and pipe and lighter I have in the breast pocket, gives me a shred of hope that I will be able to wing my way through the next few hours.

I get there and go straight to the bar and down a huge vodka. The lunch is on the second floor in a private dining room outside of which is a small bathroom. I duck into the gilded little toilet stall and scramble to pack the stem. My hands are shaking, as it's been over twenty minutes since I took my last hit at the hotel and I can barely keep the flame steady. I inhale and hold it until my lungs sting and cough out the smoke. I wash my hands and rinse my mouth with soap to hide the smell and blow on the stem to cool it before wrapping it in toilet paper and putting it in my suit pocket.

The room has a long table, with flowers and bound galleys of the book arranged beautifully. People apparently have just sat down. There has been a sort of mingling with cocktails before the lunch, so luckily I haven't been as obviously absent as I would have been if they had sat down at one o'clock. Jean stands as I walk in the door. *I just got here! I'm so sorry I was late!* she coos. So Jean doesn't even know that I'm late. Another miracle. Somehow I talk to the author, her Legendary Editor, and a few others and sit down at the table, next to Jean, and the event glides on without my help and with no apparent controversy over my lateness. I tell everyone I have the flu and am not feeling well. I make up a story for Jean about some trouble in my family that I had to attend to, and she shivers with genuine concern. I excuse myself twice during the lunch to slam glasses of vodka at the bar downstairs and duck into the toilet to smoke. I say good-bye to everyone around three thirty, wander out onto Fifth Avenue, and when I see a man in his thirties handing out flyers for some discount men's store, I recognize something in him and ask him if he parties. When he says yes, I ask, *With rock?* He flashes a smile and laughs more than says, *Oh boy.*

I won't remember this guy's name, but we become fast friends. We hunt for a cab together to get back to the hotel on 24th Street but can't find one. A van pulls up next to me as it stops for a light, and I ask the guy driving if we can hitch a ride and, amazingly, he says yes. My new pal—who has ditched his flyers in a trash can—giggles in the back of the van and for a moment he's Kenny in the woods with a bottle of Scotch, Max in the cooler setting up lines of coke, Ian wielding a fire extinguisher. I giggle, too, exhilarated to be on the other side of the lunch, on the other side of the line that separates me and my new friend from the rest of the world. The van rattles down Fifth. Drugs in pocket, partner in crime at my side, hotel key in hand, a whole night ahead.

The afternoon and night play out. We don't have sex, though I want to. Rico comes at ten with more, and it is all gone by four in the morning. My pal gets restless and disappears. He asks for $50 for a cab up to Harlem and I give him $40. Alone, I smoke down the few crumbs I'd hidden. Alone, I scrape the broken stem for the last resin and burn the pipe black as charcoal trying to suck the last drop of venom out of it. Alone, I look at the window and wonder if I am high enough up to die if I crawl through and jump into the air shaft. Fourth floor. Not even close.

And then, because there is no other thought or action or crack crumb left to get in the way, I think one thought: Noah. I can't bear it and I pick up the last burnt stem from the ashtray to make sure there is nothing left. I scan the floor to see if there is one last dropped chunk of drug kicked to the carpet's edge, waiting for me to rescue it so that it can rescue me. But there is nothing. Not a thing left but me and the knowledge that I have not called Noah in three days. It's seven in the morning and I'm alone in a hotel room on the other end of a three-day crack binge. I'm in unfamiliar territory, terrified. I feel as if I have been picked up by a tornado and spit out in pieces. Why did I drink so much at L'acajou three nights ago? WHY, oh, Jesus Christ, WHY? I've asked myself the question hundreds of times in the harsh light of hundreds of mornings and, as always, there's no answer. I pick up the mess, gather my few belongings, and walk down Fifth Avenue in the dark, silent morning, toward what I hope is still home.

Noah is not at the apartment when I come in. I call and leave a message to say that I am at the apartment, in bed, and safe. That I am sorry and that this is the last time. That I love him. I crash asleep for what seems like a few minutes but is actually three or four hours. Noah wakes me sometime after morning. He has tears in his eyes and speaks in kinder tones than I could possibly have hoped for. He hugs me as I lie in the bed and pats my back like a child who needs consoling. He looks worried and I know something is not quite right. *There are some people here to see you,* he says, and I know right away that, after all this time, all these nights and mornings, the jig is finally up. *Who?* I ask, and he tells me that my sister Kim, David, and Kate are in the living room. The world stands still. Time stops. I can't believe they know. That they're here. Noah holds my hand and I am grateful for his tenderness. That he is not leaving me. But the horror of what is happening thunders down on me, and I am numb with shock. *Let's go,* he prods. And with his help I put on my bathrobe and shuffle toward the door from the bedroom into the living room. Noah has his hand on my shoulder as I open the door and see them sitting around the coffee table in the sun-flooded living room, looking up, seeing me for the first time.

I don't struggle, not yet. I am quiet and cooperative as each of them, in turn—Kim, Kate, Noah, David—tells me they will support my getting sober but won't support me, won't have anything to do with me, if I continue to use. There are many tears and I feel that I'm underwater and their words seem as if they have to swim a great distance to reach me. There is a car downstairs, tickets purchased to fly to a rehab in Oregon, bags packed, and a bed waiting. The ex-cop or ex–Army Green Beret or ex-gym teacher who stands alongside them with muscles and crossed arms and barks at me in stern tones is someone I instinctively know to erase. I do not look at or speak to or interact with him in any way and I agree to go to the airport as long as he does not come with us. And so we go. Noah, Kate, and I get in the car and go to La Guardia. It is early afternoon, and when we get to the terminal, I say I need food and order a plate of eggs and a bottle of white wine and drink it all and barely touch the food. I drink vodka on the flight to Oregon while Noah and Kate look on silently or sleep.

The place is an hour away from Portland and looks like a small elementary school nestled in the middle of rolling wine country. It does not rain once when I am there, and the sky is a dark, unsullied blue that turns pink toward the end of the day and scarlet at sunset. My roommate is a pill-addicted brain surgeon from Los

Angeles whose gorgeous Swedish girlfriend comes up several times and takes us on car rides to Portland and to the coast. There are other guys, too — the retired ambulance driver from Washington State who drank himself into a stupor every night and who would go weeks without a word to another human being; the mouthy rich kid from New York who wore gold Adidas track suits and talked like a mobster; the spooked meth addict from the San Fernando Valley who lined his basement with aluminum foil to outsmart the Feds and cops who he just knew were tracking his every movement. I relate to them all. On the second or third day, after dozens of pleading phone calls to Noah and Kate and my sister, each one a failed attempt to get back to New York, I finally accept the fact that I am in rehab, that I am stuck. Once I stop trying to get home, I am amazed how at ease with these guys I feel, how much the same, and how exhilarating it is to be honest, about everything, for the first time. Each night I walk alone in a gentle field and watch the sky darken and streak with pinks and reds. I walk in that field and feel scared about returning to New York, worry what people will think, but after a few weeks begin to feel hopeful.

I volunteer to stay for an extra week — partly because I want to demonstrate to Noah and Kate that I have taken this seriously, but mostly because by the fourth week I am deeply enmeshed in the community of patients and counselors. I am not in a hurry to leave this process of letting go of the many secrets that I had spent a lifetime squirreling away, hanging on to, buckling under the weight of.

In a group discussion one morning I talk, for the first time since the sessions with Dr. Dave, about my struggle with peeing. After the group, another guy, a banker from San Francisco with four kids, tells me that he wrestled with the same problem as a boy. Two days before I go home, he will sneak off the rehab property, relapse on tequila in a strip club down the road, and be asked to leave.

When I return to New York, my mother calls and wants to see me. I put off getting together for nearly a month and eventually agree to have lunch. On that day she is an hour and a half late. She finally shows up and as we order food, she describes the generations of alcoholism and drug addiction in her family and my father's, and tells me I'm one in a long line. Despite my initial agitation with her for being late, I am surprisingly relaxed with her and feel a little of our old ease return. I ask if I can bring up something from childhood, something that I hadn't talked to anyone in the family about but that I've remembered only recently. She says yes and before I get the word *peeing* out of my mouth, she holds her hand up above the table and shakes her head. I say a few more words, but she is now crying, asking me if I've agreed to have lunch only to tell her what a terrible mother she is. Stunned by her sudden outburst, I say that I only need her to tell me if she remembers anything, to confirm that it happened, because all I have are a pile of chaotic memories shaken to life by a shrink. Through tears she says something that sounds like *I'm not going to talk about that, your father was the one*... The last thing I remember is her asking me if I knew how hard it was for her then, what a nightmare those years were for her. I say yes, that she's been very good at letting us know how hard it was for her, and she leaves the restaurant. I follow her out to the street as she disappears into a cab without a word. I return to the restaurant, settle the bill, and by the time I make my way three blocks north to my office, I lose my wallet, my keys, and my sunglasses.

I start an outpatient program that I never finish, follow the suggestions to stay sober that I was given at rehab and then don't, talk on the phone a few times to my roommate and some of the other guys — the ones who just weeks before felt like family — and then, within the first month at home, lose touch with them all.

I think I have it licked. I throw myself into my job, the agency, the writers I represent, and the storm of work seems like something that I can hide in, that will protect me from temptation. I watch people drink at dinners and parties and, at first, am relieved I don't have to anymore. As months pass, though, I grow resentful. Little fantasies of getting high will start to appear like thought bubbles in cartoons, when I am alone, mainly, and at the end of long workdays, days when I have had little sleep the night before or missed lunch and am light-headed with hunger. In October I find an old crack pipe stuffed in the pocket of a blazer hanging in our bedroom closet. I hide it in various places and circle the thing like a hawk for weeks until I finally scrape it clean of its old residue and take a hit. I feel only the faintest gust of a high, which quickly dies with the panic that I've relapsed. It's over just as it starts, and Noah walks in right after it happens and agrees to tell no one. I hide the stem, bring it to my office, and somehow misplace it. I worry for weeks

that someone there—my assistant, Kate, the cleaning woman—
has found it and is waiting to confront me. No one ever does.

And then, seven months later, just before going to Park City,
Utah, for the Sundance Film Festival, I have a plan to meet Noah
for a sushi dinner at Japonica. On the morning of the day before
that dinner, the thought of getting high bubbles up, but instead of
flicking it away as I usually do, this time I don't and it lingers. And
it lingers long enough for me to ask: Why not? Noah is leaving
tomorrow and I'll have almost two full days in the city alone. I've
been working hard, everything is going well, no one will suspect
a thing. Within seconds I'm on my cell phone, calling Stephen for
the first time in almost a year. We'd stopped using him to bartend
our parties, but despite being advised at rehab to erase all drug-
related numbers from my cell phone, I still have his. He picks up
on the first ring and we make a plan to meet later, on the corner
outside my office building. At six I go downstairs and see him
leaning against the building. He's skinnier than I remembered,
older. I barely say hello, though he seems eager to hang out. I give
him $400 to score and $200 for doing the dirty work and agree
to meet him the next day. As much as I don't want to reconnect
with Stephen, scoring through him somehow feels less wrong. As
long as I don't start up with the dealers again, I reason, if I don't
remember their numbers, this tiny treat will be just a one-time-
only thing, an anomaly, a harmless but needed vacation.

I meet Stephen on the same corner the next day, tingling with
anticipation. This time he's all business. He hands me a small

brown paper bag filled with drugs and stems. I thank him and hurry away, back to my office.

I plan to smoke the bags the next night, after Noah leaves, a day and a half before I join him in Utah for the premiere of his movie. This can work, I think, this will be just a little release, a little nothing, a harmless blowing off of steam. In the swarm of faulty reasoning I still know this will end badly, that it always does, and that I'm loading a gun and pointing it at my temple. But that voice, instead of being a deterrent, becomes part of the persuasion. On the other side of this bag is either a groggy day and a no-harm-done return to life or some kind of apocalypse. Lose nothing or lose everything. And losing everything sounds like a relief.

I return to the office and make some phone calls, say good-bye to my colleagues as they leave, and see that I have two hours before I'm to meet Noah for dinner. Two hours. Just one hit now would wear off before then. Why not? I get up from my desk and lock the office door. I find a lighter in my assistant's desk drawer, sit down at my desk, take the drugs from my jacket pocket, and hold the two little baggies in my hand. I pull out the clean, clear stem — so much lighter than I remembered. It feels like a dream as I split off a little creamy chunk of crack and load it into the end of the stem. It doesn't seem as if it's actually happening when I spark the lighter and move the flame toward the pipe. It doesn't feel the least bit wrong in those first seconds after exhaling the familiar smoke, no more than a reunion with an old friend, a returning to the most incredible conversation I've ever had, one that got interrupted seven months ago and, now that it's started up again, hasn't skipped a beat. But it's more than just a conversation, it's the best sex, the most delicious meal, the most engrossing book—it's like returning to all of these at once, coming home, and the primary feeling I have as I collapse back into my desk chair and watch the smoke roll through my office is: *Why on earth did I ever leave?*

I sit at my desk for three hours, smoking down one of the bags, and finally race out, suddenly panicked, to Japonica, to Noah, whom I was supposed to meet an hour ago. I run into the restaurant and see him sitting at a table, his back to the wall, clearly worried, and when he sees me, he goes white and begins weeping. I remember his weeping. I lie to him and say I got caught on a phone call at work, that I didn't hear him ringing my cell or the landline at the office, and that it's all okay, don't worry, stop crying. He sleeps on the couch that night and leaves quietly in the morning, asking only one thing: Will I make it to Sundance? And I say, yes, yes, of course. I promise.

And I do make it. But I stay only one night, the night of his premiere and the party after with his friends and producers and family. I smile and nod and engage and play the part of a supportive boyfriend. But I'm fixated on the little zip-lock bag wrapped in tissue nestled in the pocket of my navy blazer hanging in the bedroom closet at One Fifth. I imagine the clear glass stem resting next to that bag, and the lighter on the dresser nearby. I picture these things every second I'm in Utah. From the moment I get there I need to leave. From the second I leave New York I need to return, to get back to that conversation, the one that just started up again; and now that it has, nothing but death can keep me from it.

Last Door

I need a new sweater. I need to clean up before I try to check into
another hotel. It is evening but some stores may still be open. I get
in a cab and ask the driver to go to SoHo. He hums as he drives
and I can't bear looking to see if his license photo is obscured by
cardboard or paper or just not there, like all the others. *Here okay?*
he asks, as he pulls to the corner of Houston and Wooster. I shove
$10 in the money slot and don't bother looking at the fare.

The stores south of Houston look like Christmas. Extraordinary
displays — animated, art-directed, intelligently lit — beckon and
intimidate from the windows along Wooster. I remember, as a kid,
coming into the city with my fourth- or fifth-grade class to see the
Radio City Music Hall Christmas show. The streets in midtown
were jammed with tourists and city people, and they were lined
up by the hundreds to see the decorated windows of Saks Fifth

Avenue and Lord & Taylor. I remember being confused about why the windows were important to see but also excited that I was involved in something famous, something big. It was the same feeling when we got to Radio City Music Hall. My mother told me it was the best theater in the whole world and that the Rockettes were the most beautiful, most talented performers anywhere, whom people came from around the world to see. When my class finally made its way through the crowds into Radio City I could barely breathe. We were here, in this place that people traveled from everywhere to be, where the Rockettes performed (what exactly they did I still had no idea). The gold fixtures and red carpeting exaggerated the dizzy Christmas-in-NY adrenaline pumping through me, and I remember literally shaking with excitement. At the top of the first set of stairs, there was a bank of pay phones. I made a beeline for the nearest one and dialed zero. I told the operater I wanted to call home, collect. The phone rang and no one answered. This was before answering machines. Before voice mail. So I hung up. But I was bursting and had to tell someone, had to put the excitement somewhere. So I picked up the phone and dialed the operator again — a different one answered this time — and immediately started gushing to her about where I was, what I could see, what I had already seen on this, one of my first trips into the city. I don't remember anything about the performance that night but I always remember that call, the friendly operator, her kind voice, and how she told me to go find my teacher, to be careful not to get lost.

I wander past the bright, contrived windows along Wooster and try to remember what time of year it is. It looks like Christmas but I'm sure it's not. It takes longer than a few beats to remember that it's March. I make my way into a wide, light, serene store, with low tables and discreet racks hanging with what look to be carefully curated garments. I ask a dark-haired saleswoman with eyes like opals — blue with flashing gold and red — if they have any men's turtleneck sweaters. I tell her I'm visiting and have run the one I'm wearing into the ground. She looks down my torso at what I am wearing, and her frown and wrinkled brow seem to agree. She directs me down a flight of steps to the lower level. Near the bottom of the stairs is a small basket of folded cashmere turtlenecks, and I pick the smallest one they have, in burgundy, with a cable knit pattern, and find a changing room. The moment the door clicks shut, I pack a thick hit, cough loudly to mask the sound of the lighter, and hungrily draw from the stem. I blow the smoke wide and close my eyes for a few minutes. I have no idea where I will go next and I lean against the back of the changing room wall and let the warm glow of the drug shield me from caring. This little changing room, nothing more than a cube of light and mirror and white paint, is safe, and for a moment I am calm.

I slump further down the wall and let every tense, clenched muscle loosen. It feels as if each limb, every digit, could fall off. The contraption of my body feels barely assembled, on the verge of collapse. Out of nowhere comes a memory of Noah weeping at Japonica. Shaking his head and sobbing. Telling me not to explain, not to say another word, that he knew I was high, could see it on every inch of me.

I pack a hit as big and as fast as I possibly can. It takes a few deep draws for the vision of Noah to dim, and after a few more hits the exorcism is complete. The tiny changing room is thick with smoke, and I know I need to leave. After another big hit, I suddenly remember the SoHo Grand Hotel, which can't be far and where, thankfully, I have no history.

I sit up and shimmer with the promise of a clean, new hotel room as more smoke curls around the ceiling of the changing cubicle. Energized now with a plan, finally a place I can go, I cool off the lighter and stem and head back into the store. As I walk, I notice that my jeans won't stay up anymore. My old blue cashmere sweater is tucked in all around my waist, but the soiled, worn-thin Levis are still slipping off me. I need to get a new hole punched in my belt before going to the hotel.

The downstairs of the store is brighter now than I remembered, and smaller. I worry they've been listening to me get high and that they can smell the smoke pouring from the now open door of the changing room. Without trying on the sweater, I race upstairs to the opal-eyed woman and tell her I'd like to buy it. She runs my debit card through and as she pulls out the bag that has the words *Christopher Fischer* scrawled across its meridian, I look around the store. Where once it had a sleek impenetrable chic, it now has a slapped-together, flimsy quality. The bag looks odd, too thick, too bright, too big, as if it were a prop bag for some off-Broadway play that involved shopping. The opal-eyed woman folds the sweater in a confection of tissue, places it in the phony bag, and hands me my receipt as she tells me to have a nice evening. I can feel my grip on reality loosen as I take the bag. Is this some setup? But how would they know I'd come here? I rush out of the store and onto Wooster Street.

A few beats later I hear my name being called in a high-pitched, nervous, southern accent. *Bill, oh, hello, Bill.* I freeze. *ROSIE?!* Old art-project, crack-smoking, 23rd Street Rosie? What's she doing here? Jesus, is she in on this? I look around and can't see anyone I know. My heart pounds and my neck chokes with a sudden rush of blood to my head. And there she is: Barbara. A lovely middle-aged, impeccably dressed woman who acts as an adviser to foreign publishing houses, what people in publishing call a scout. I've known her, not well, for years. She eyes me with worry, but kindly, and quickly I say hello and move on before a conversation can take root. Seeing her jolts me into thinking about book publishing, the agency, Kate, our employees, my writers — Jesus, all those writers. And with them the names and faces and voices of all the publishers, editors, agents, scouts, publicists, and assistants roar to life, one by one, like a great, animated mural — scolding and disgusted. And then, again, memories of rehab and Noah flood back in. With my fake shopping bag in one hand and debit card in the other, I start hustling west toward the SoHo Grand.

I see — oh, dear God, thank you — a leather shop and immediately go in, take off my belt, and ask to have a few new holes punched. This is the third time I have done this in the last five weeks. At one point, in some hotel room, I have taken a knife and stabbed out a new, albeit rougher, hole. The old guy behind the stack of bags and wallets eyes the weathered belt and me cautiously and says, *You're going to need more than just a few.* He makes three and when I put the belt on it links, easily, to the last one. I consider having him make another, but judging by how quickly he makes the holes and rings up the price, it seems he wants me gone. I walk for a few blocks toward the hotel, but before I get there I know I need to change out of my mangy blue sweater. I've been wearing it for over a month. It's stretched out of shape and the unidentifiable residue that crusts and streaks along the neck and chest is, I'm worried but not exactly sure, beginning to smell.

A few blocks away, I see a small Chinese restaurant. It's the kind with only three or four tables that is mostly for takeout. There are no other customers in the store when I enter. I step up to the counter and ask if I can use the bathroom, and the boy there, no more than sixteen, says that it's for customer use only. A woman I assume is his mother joins him and repeats that it's not for public use.

I am desperate to change and also getting antsy for a hit, so I order three dishes and some egg rolls for takeout and ask, a little impatiently, if I can use the bathroom *now*. The woman says, yes, if I pay first. So I do. I walk past the counter to the back of the kitchen, where there is a tiny bathroom. Luckily it has a window and a mirror. I run the water and flush the toilet to mask the sounds of the clicking lighter and the popping sound the drug makes when it's lit. I pack the stem and light up. I load it again, since I'm feeling far from relieved after the first hit. The rock pops at the end of the stem when I pull, and the glass at the very end cracks apart. This sometimes happens when you put a big cold chunk of crack in a still-hot stem and light up too quickly. I scramble as quietly as I can to clean up the small bits of glass, find the thank-God-still-intact rock of crack, and reload the broken stem. My agitation is high, so I pack in even more. The hit is big and I blow the smoke out the window and, thankfully, begin to feel a wash of relief as I exhale. I wriggle out of my sweater and see my torso in the little mirror. Ribs and bones jut everywhere, and the color of my skin is light gray. Little scrapes and burn marks and scabs speckle my arms, chest, and stomach. I feel, for the first time, beyond the desire for sex, as if I have passed into another state of being high, where sex no longer matters. I am relieved, because the body in the mirror is not one I would want anyone to see. I look more closely at the worst burn marks and cuts, the ones on my hands and forearms, and I shudder. I look in the mirror again and see how little skin I have, how my frame seems covered by the thinnest sheet, pulled tight. I look like I crawled out of a fire, starving. I have never seen my pelvic bones winging from my abdomen in the way they do now and I'm relieved, as I pull the sweater over my head, that this glorious, thick miracle of costly fabric covers all of it. I wash my face and hands, wipe away various stains on my jeans, and pick lint and hair and detritus from the rim of my trusty cap. I find Visine in my jacket and drown my eyes in it. I wash my mouth out with soap and rub it under my armpits to cover up whatever odor may be coming from there. I fire up another blast, blow on the stem, wrap it up, put the old sweater in the bag, and open the door that leads to the kitchen and the front of the shop. There are two men — heavy-jacketed, dull-panted, gray-shoed

Penneys — and they are looking directly at me as I step toward the counter. The food is in bags, ready, and I grab them, thank the woman and the boy, and leave. As I walk west, I turn back and see the two Penneys exit the restaurant and begin walking my way. I change directions several times, and after twenty or so minutes I think I've lost them. I throw the Chinese food and the shopping bag with my old sweater into a garbage can. My heart is racing and I'm worried that I'll be too panicky to make it through the check-in process at the front desk of the SoHo Grand. I'm too jumpy to stop at a bar and get a drink, so I decide to just go for it. Just get to the room. Once there, I will be okay. Once there, I can order room service, call Happy, drink bottles of vodka to take the sharp edges off. I am focused on the short-term relief of the hotel room, but under everything is a creeping knowledge that with not much money left, not much more weight to lose, and not many more places to hide, this is it. An end of some kind is near.

I stop by a deli around the corner from the hotel and get ten lighters, six boxes of sleeping pills, and a six-pack of beer so that I have something to drink the second I get to the room. I wish I could take a hit before going into the hotel, but I know it's now or never. I head into the new brick-and-glass building, and as I march, as slowly and calmly as I can, up the steps, I think of the clean sheets, the gushing shower, the room service, the immaculate surfaces, the safety. The place is crawling with guys who look like production assistants on movies — all hats and jeans and scruff. Thank God. Thank God I don't stick out. Instantly I imagine I am in town from L.A. on a shoot and that anyone noticing my weight, the rings under my bloodshot eyes, the greasy hair poking out from my cap, will just chalk it up to a tight production schedule and late nights in the editing room going over the dailies. So with this fantasy flickering behind my movements, I go to the front desk and ask for a room. *How many nights?* the woman asks, and I make a quick calculation of the $500 room rate and the amount of crack I plan on buying from Happy. I tell her four nights and that I need to check in under an alias as well as needing a smoking room. She doesn't skip a beat. She says, *Fine,* runs my debit card, looks at my passport, hands me a plastic room card, and off I go. I practically giggle from excitement and relief in the elevator as I'm heading up to what is the third floor from the top of the building. I clock that it's high enough for a jump to matter. If all else fails, there is that.

The room is small, on the southwest corner, and dimly lit. The lights of SoHo, Tribeca, and Wall Street dance and blink on the other side of the large windows, and it feels, when I first step into the room, like being on the inside of a snow globe suspended in midair, high above the city. I stand at the window and call Happy for the last time.

He arrives around one. I'd smoked down what I had left from the bag at Rosie's an hour ago, and my stem is now less than two inches long, caked with burnt, unsmokable residue. When I called hours earlier I asked for $2,000 worth. More than I've ever ordered. I can only give him $1,500 in cash—what was left of my limit when I went to the ATM before midnight and a new grand after. I ask him, this one time, to sport me the difference. He pauses, briefly, and starts counting out the bags and new stems. *Nice hotel,* he says, commenting for the first time ever on where I'm staying. *Nice room.* And he leaves. Looking at the forty bags of crack on my bedspread, the most I have ever seen in one place, makes me feel safer than I have felt all day. The bags look fuller, more jam-packed than usual, and the abundance, the dancing light outside the window, and the awareness that I will never leave this room sends a high through my system before I even light up. I lie down on the bed and drop the bags on my chest and face, one by one, and then all at once. It feels like an arrival. The end of a jour-ney. Not just the panicked one of days and nights and weeks after relapsing, but the long one, the whole useless struggle. The lines from that novel rise up again, but this time with new meaning. *It would be now.*

I pull the curtains shut and pack a hit with one of the new stems and, more than ever before, let the crumbs scatter about. It won't matter. I won't see the end of this pile. There is no way I can survive this. I pack another hit. Another. And another. Happy has given me eight stems, and I load two more so I don't have to wait for one to cool before I start the next. I inhale smoke nonstop for nearly an hour, naked and breathing more smoke than air. I am filled with smoke — warm, electric, big. I feel weightless in this dim room. I am almost nothing. I am, finally, about to be nothing.

I order bottles and bottles of vodka from room service, no food. I smoke and drink all night, and by morning I have gone through a third of what I bought from Happy and panic that I won't have enough. By midnight, I decide to get $1,000 from the ATM and call Rico and ask him to float me a grand's worth until the next day. I've never asked Rico for an advance but he doesn't hesitate. When he comes around two in the morning—heavyset, cranky, and in a bulky red sweatshirt—he throws in a couple hundred extra, in addition to the thousand on credit. *On the house. Eat something, man,* he says, and for a moment he looks worried. But only for a moment and then he's gone. I gather all the little bags together. A bigger pile than the night before and now, with only $4,000 in my account and a hotel bill ticking up, I worry, again, if I will have enough. Death and an empty bank account are racing neck and neck, and it's the former I am pinning everything on.

I take all the sleeping pills out of their boxes and pop each one free from the thick sheets of safety packaging. I put the pills in a clear water glass from the bathroom and empty all the crack into another. My hands shake as I move the pills and the crack, and my whole body rocks in time with my heartbeat. I am drinking vodka like water and nervous each time I have to order another couple bottles that the room-service boys will report to the desk that there is something funny going on in my room.

The second morning comes on and the room seems smaller. I open the curtains and the day outside is gray, still. I am looking out the window at neighborhoods I've eaten and shopped and walked in for years, and yet I feel as if I'm seeing a city I've never been to. Nothing appears familiar and it seems less like a place I could go down the elevator and visit, and more like a photograph or a mural I can only regard.

I continue to smoke and am grateful for a ventilation system that draws the billowing clouds away as soon as I exhale. I have kept a window cracked to allow fresh air in, and for once I don't worry about the smell seeping down the hall to alert other guests or hotel employees.

I stand at the window, towel around my waist, and notice across the lot behind the hotel a string of black SUVs and several dark sedans lined up in a row. There must be nine of them, and I think but am not sure I see two people sitting in the front seat of each. I stop breathing. One of them seems to be holding a pair of binoculars. My heart begins to slam in my chest. It looks as if they all have binoculars. Eighteen pairs of them, trained directly on this window, this room, me. My towel slips off and I drop to my knees and kneel up to the window. One of them is waving. It's hard to tell but I'm sure he's waving from behind the glass. There's a reflection, but yes, yes, his arm is waving. Fuck, they're all waving. Waving with one hand and holding binoculars in the other. I feel like I've been electrocuted. My arms and neck ache, and I think I'm having a heart attack. Fuck, fuck, fuck, fuck, FUCK! I shout to myself as I pace the room and pour a full glass of vodka, downing it in one gulp. FUCK. I immediately grab a new stem and jam it full. SHIT! I scream as I stop myself from lighting up. I can't smoke it with the curtains open. Not with them all watching. But I can't close them, they'll storm the room. Oh, my God, they are going to storm the room. I run to the bathroom and turn on the shower to hide the sound of the lighter and the loud popping sound of the flame scorching the too-large chunk of crack at the end of the stem. It takes three long pulls to smoke the stem down, and I grab a towel and lay it across the base of the door to the room. Suddenly I notice that the ventilation system in the bathroom isn't very good. The smoke hangs heavy and slow in the air at the top of the ceiling. I open the door and return to the room. Without looking out the window, I close the curtains, sit down on the bed, load up the stem, and smoke. And again. And again. I am low on vodka and without it I will shake out of control. After a few moments pass, I do it again. I'm terrified now of calling downstairs for more, but I do. I grab shampoo and streak the walls around the bathroom door and the vents of the air system, hoping to create a fresh smell. I drink the last of the vodka, load up more hits, and look at my watch and see that it's after one o'clock. I have one more night left in the hotel and I know there is not enough money in my account for another. The vodka comes, and the boy who delivers it is not a boy but a man and too smooth, I think, too in control, and too, well, manly to be a room-service waiter. Fuck, I think. Undercover. I thank him, sign the bill, and when he asks if there's anything else, I think, GET THE FUCK OUT! but gently say, *No thanks*, and keep my shaking hands behind my back. He leaves and I think I hear something above me. Is there another room above me or the roof? I can't remember. I pace the room, light a hit, and decide whether to open the curtains and look up. It takes forty-five minutes and nearly half a bottle of vodka for me to pull back the curtains, lean out, look up, and notice that there is an open roof above this room and not another room. The building steps back at the top, and my floor is the last before it narrows. I look out

across the lot to the line of black SUVs and sedans and think I see
the flash of a lighter go off in one. And another. Are they trying to
drive me insane? Why are they watching me? Why don't they just
arrest me? WHO THE FUCK ARE THEY? I suddenly feel light,
flimsy. Defenseless. I try to stand but stay bent with dread, like
a half-closed jackknife. I close the curtains and crouch on tiptoes
back to the bed. The noises above—footfalls? Something drag-
ging? Are they planning on scaling down from the roof and coming in through the windows? I realize how small this room is and
wonder if they've rigged it this way solely for me—is it usually
part of a larger suite, but when they saw me coming, they created
a wired, camera equipped, roof-accessible space to corner me into
a bust? A radio sounds from somewhere—in the hall? The roof?
I jump off the bed toward the dresser. My towel comes off again,
and I see in the mirror a rickety skeleton—elbows and knees and
knuckles bulging like bolted wooden joints strung with thread. I
am the marionette I have seen hundreds of times before but never
thought was me. I am only sticks and strings and spasms. Money
gone. Love gone. Career gone. Reputation gone. Friends gone.
Hope gone. Compassion gone. Usefulness gone. Second chances
gone. And if there had been any hesitation about dying, that's gone
now, too. I take a huge hit. There must be almost $2,000 worth of
crack left in the glass cup. I have almost two full bottles of vodka,
a water glass full of sleeping pills, two clean and three rough-but-
usable stems left. I need to get it all down as fast as possible, to wal-
lop my system hard enough before anyone breaks into the room.
I've slept only a handful of hours over the last six weeks. I cannot remember eating. I'm sure my racked body won't survive if
I overwhelm it with what I have. The team of binocular-holding,
lighter-flashing, hand-waving SUV drivers outside, who now seem

to be on the roof, are, at any second, it seems, about to explode through the door and windows.

As fast as I can, I put on my boxer shorts. It is suddenly, urgently, important to have boxers on and for everything to be clean. If the room gets stormed, I don't want it streaked with residue and mess and I don't want to be naked. I wipe down the surfaces of the bathroom and the bedroom and gather the glasses with the pills and the crack next to the bed. I set up the bottles of vodka on the floor and bring an empty one to pee into. At some point during the cleaning and gathering I decide that once I lie down on the bed I will not leave it. I sit at its edge and pack a hit. I smoke hit after hit, but it seems I can't make a dent in the pile of drugs in the glass. I begin to take the pills. One after another, with big mouthfuls of vodka. I hear footsteps on the roof. The sound of ropes, of heavy boots, of cables. Boxes piled with guns scraping the concrete. Surveillance equipment being hauled. More footsteps. More hits. More pills and larger gulps of vodka. This goes on and on in the half-lit room, the late morning sun seeping through the closed curtains. The surfaces that had once seemed to shimmer with the most inviting urban glamour now look cheap and cold and ordinary. I hear a helicopter and imagine the men above fastening the roof with cables lowered from a large, powerful chopper that will—any second now—lift the little cube of a room into the air, away from the city, and behind the walls of a federal prison. The bed feels as if it is rocking, and I cannot tell if it is me, the bed, or the entire room. I down more pills. I smoke more. Drink more. Find a piece of paper and, as Noah wrote so many times on the back of envelopes and left on the bar in our foyer, write *Can't take it,* and leave it next to the bed. I can barely move my arms, and my legs begin to ache. My heart feels like it is a rocket taking off from inside my chest, but at the same time a low, dull wave of drowsy energy begins to roll at the back of my neck and head.

The pills are nearly gone. I wonder, for the first time, if I really want to go through with this. There still might be a chance to crawl up and out of this deep well. Do I really want to die? I stop and the sounds on the roof stop, too. Everything is silent but for the roaring of blood behind my eyes and ears and chest. All I can hear is life slamming through my tired, aching body. Do I want to do this? Now? The sound of something snapping comes from the roof and I startle.

Yes, I think as I lean over to pick up the glass with the pills and slide the last ten or so into my mouth. *Yes,* I say out loud to the men on the roof and the ones in the vans who must be listening. *YES,* I shout, before I chug the dregs of vodka from the bottle. *Yes,* I whisper angrily, packing the only clean stem until it bulges. Yes and Yes and Yes as I finish it all and my limbs slow and the great drowsy, long-awaited wave rises, crests and, at last, crashes down. Yes.

For a long time, the next thing I remembered was being in the lobby of One Fifth, holding on to the front desk, telling Luis that I needed the new key. But over time I remember standing on the northeast corner of Fifth Avenue and Washington Square Park. Did a cab leave me here? Did I walk from the hotel? I had no idea then and have no idea now. But I remember standing at the corner, not knowing what to do. Whether to go home or not. I have no money. Nothing. And I can barely stay awake. I can lie down on the sidewalk and sleep so easily. If I can just find a spot, out of the way, where I won't get arrested or harassed. Sleep is on me like the heaviest blanket, and I can't stand still without stumbling. I start walking north up Fifth, toward home.

And so Luis—thirty-something, extremely polite, Hispanic, the same doorman I have waved hello to coming in and out of the lobby for years—is telling me that Noah is not at home and that I'm not allowed in the building. He says it nicely, but he says it. I ask him to just please give me the new key. I tell him it will be fine, Noah won't mind. He tells me he's been instructed not to give it to me, and I tell him if I don't lie down somewhere I will die. I can now barely stand up. He calls John, the building manager. John comes down and asks me to follow him. We go to the second floor, where he has a small office, and he suggests I wait with him until Noah gets back. I tell him he has to call Noah. My cell phone is dead. He dials the number and hands me the phone. Noah's voice mail picks up, and I tell him I'm home and they won't let me in. At some point during the message I fall down. My legs give out and I'm on the floor in front of John's desk. He helps me up, but there is nowhere to sit. I hang on to the door frame behind me. I am awake and asleep, alive and dead, and I don't know how I got here. John is talking, and I'm no longer hearing his words. His phone rings and he puts it to my ear. It's Noah. *Hi,* I say. *I'm home. Help. Please.* I give the phone to John and more sounds happen and then John is walking me downstairs, to Luis's desk. Give him the key, John says, and Luis opens the cabinet to get it. There is some confusion about old and new keys, but eventually a key ends up in my hand and I start heading for the elevator. When I get in, I can't remember what floor we lived on. Three? I hit three and know it's not right. Five? Six? Six. Six. Six W. So I hit six. The doors open and close on three, and for a moment I forget it's not my floor and move toward the door. I remember, but when I stop, my body buckles again and I'm on the floor. The doors shut and I manage to stand up as the doors open on six. The apartment is to the right of the elevator, the last door on the left. I start toward the door and hang on to the wall the whole way. I finally get there and see the shiny new steel lock where the old copper-colored one had been. I don't know what I've done with the key and as I search my pockets I realize it's still in my right hand. Now I just need to open the door. But I can't seem to guide the key into the lock. It must be the wrong one. Maybe we live on the seventh floor. Maybe the fourth. I keep poking at the lock, but my hand is shaking and I can't make it go in. Now that I've stopped walking, the drowsiness hits like a tidal wave. I'm leaning against the wall next to the door, but I can't stay up. I'm going down and hold on to the knob to keep from falling backwards. I sway in place for a while, and as it all begins to go dark, there are hands at my back, along my arms, taking the key, pulling me up. I see them on my wrists, and they are the most beautiful things I've ever seen. Made of light, not flesh, winging around me with good purpose and grace. Noah. He pulls me against him — he smells like dry cleaning and cigarettes — helps me stay up with one hand and unlocks the door with the other. He is speaking but the words are too far away. He tries to hold me up as the door opens but I'm already down. The light from the apartment streaks toward us. I fall in.

White Plains

An ambulance will wait by the service entrance at One Fifth to take me to Lenox Hill Hospital. Unlike the ride to the hospital when I am twelve, this one won't be remembered — there will be no surfacing between awake and unawake, no comforting voices. I won't remember the emergency room, won't remember the elevator to the psych ward, won't remember anything beyond falling through the apartment door, Noah behind me, the light.

I wake in a room, alone, strapped to a bed, with no idea where I am. It takes several minutes to register that I am alive, and when it does, I am furious. Nurses come. A doctor. People — my family, Noah — are outside the door, but I tell the nurses not to let anyone in. I stay frozen, in the room, with only one thought: What now?

Julia, a friend from Los Angeles, keeps calling. Nurses come in many times a day to say she is either waiting on the pay phone line or has left another message that I should call her. She does this for days and finally, before I speak to or see anyone else, I go to the phone. I leave the bed and room for the first time and wander toward the pay phone by the nurses' station. *Hi,* I say, and she fills my ears with her words. For a while, hers are the only words I can hear and she will say them over and over and keep saying them for weeks, then months.

I am given another room. It is small, with two beds, and looks out onto a church on 77th Street. When I get to the room it is empty and there is no sign of a roommate. An enormous white orchid is sitting on the dresser. It has two tall bamboo stakes with sharp, pointy ends to support the plant. It's from Jean and there is a note that asks me to be on the board of her literary magazine — *I keep meaning to ask you,* it says as if nothing has gone on, and it closes with *So much love.* I stare at the orchid, her scrawled handwriting, the thick, creamy stationery, and wonder who it was she thought she knew, who she thought she loved. I take one of the bamboo stakes, snap it in half, and go into the bright blue-tiled bathroom and start jamming it into my wrist. I keep jamming, harder and harder, until the skin breaks and blood comes, and I look down at my fist pumping the little weapon into my arm, see how dreadful what I am doing is, and register, in that instant, that I don't want to die. Suddenly and for the first time, dying seems like the last thing I want. I stop, grateful not to have caused more damage, put my arm under cold water, rinse the wound, wrap it in paper towels, and sit on the small bed facing the window. I sit there for a long time. I look at the church steeple and wait.

Before I see anyone, most of my family return to their lives in New England. My mother stays in a friend's apartment on the Upper West Side, but I ask not to see her. Noah comes a few times and looks more handsome than I have ever seen him. He sits across a cafeteria table from me and I am both shamed and dazzled by him. I weigh just over 130 pounds, almost 40 pounds less than my usual weight, swimming in pajama bottoms and a sweatshirt, and he glows in an elegant agnès b. shirt, collared English sweater, and chic gray city coat. I remember his buying each of these things. It is never said, but it is clear that it is over, that our lives, bound together for so long, will now be lived apart. Everything that we were, the whole magical, horrible opera, is now over. We are only a table apart but we're in different worlds. He seems less like a person and more like a figment from a dream I once had, some nocturnal wonder I cannot revive after sleep, only remember.

And then Katherine appears. After waking from a nightmare where she sees me wandering in city traffic, careening between cabs and buses, she calls her father, who has just heard from someone in our small town that there is trouble. Katherine hangs up the phone, drives to the airport in Lubbock, Texas, where she is living, catches the next plane to New York, and arrives the day before I stumble home, before the ambulance comes. She sits through two weeks of visiting hours, in the hall, mostly alone, always with a book. When people come to see me, she returns to the hall, and when they leave and I am on my own, she comes back.

One afternoon, she tells me the story of a plane we planned to steal the summer between our graduating from grammar school and entering high school. It was called *The Alaskan Express*, she reminds me, and describes how we had hatched an exhaustive plan — with maps and diagrams and budgets — to fly it to a deserted island in the Caribbean. Our friend Michael, who knew how to fly from his father, who was a pilot, was part of the scheme, too. She reminds me all about it — how we planned to pack seeds to plant elaborate gardens and find equipment to convert salt water to fresh; how the three of us had figured out a way to not have to leave one another, not have to move on. I had forgotten about the plane, the whole story, how possible it all seemed then. I listen to her and feel as I did when I was ten — awed by what she knows and grateful for her attention. But mostly we don't talk. She holds my hand and we sit, in a hospital again, just as we were at the beginning, together and without words.

Two weeks later, Noah, Katherine, and I meet with the psychiatrist I've been assigned and discuss rehabs. We pick one. Katherine goes to One Fifth and packs up some of my clothes and a few books. She helps me to the street with my bags, hugs me goodbye, and returns to Texas. We will drift apart again, she will go to Belize and for months I won't hear anything, but she will resurface — a phone call, an e-mail — and the fabric will mend again, for a little while.

David, whom I haven't seen since our breakfast at Marquet, is waiting outside Lenox Hill, on the corner of 77th and Park Avenue, with his Jeep. He is both warm and cautious, and we drive, mostly in silence, to White Plains, N.Y., to the grounds of an old asylum turned into a psychiatric hospital, with a small rehab center tucked in the back. We stop at a large drugstore near the rehab, and I look at the people wandering the aisles and wonder how they live their lives, how anyone does. He walks me through the store like a father taking his son to camp, asks me if I want toothpaste, candy, notebooks. He buys me two notebooks. I will fill them.

During those first nights in White Plains, I wonder about the boy who is assigned to the room across the hall — and his worried mother, setting his things down, eyeing him as if he will take flight or disappear in a flash if she turns her back. She reminds me of Noah. And when the boy looks at me, briefly, with eyes that are two black marbles, drained of hope and color and life, I see myself.

In the evenings, I walk in a gentle, sloping field, much like the one in Oregon, and wonder what will happen next. There is one late afternoon, a few days before I return to New York, when anxiety and despair overwhelm me and I get on my knees at the top of the field. It's wet from rain earlier in the day and the sky is lightless and gray with fog. I lie down in the damp and muddy grass and whisper into the soil for help. I do this for a long time and at some point stand up, pants soaked at the knees and thighs, hands and elbows caked with mud. When I stand, I see a small break in the wall of cloud and through it a faint streak of light. It is pale and pink and the most beautiful thing I have ever seen. The cloud opens wider, the light grows, and as it does, I feel an easing. I know, if only for that moment, that my worry will change nothing and that everything is as it's supposed to be. That I will be okay.

I walk down the field as night falls. When I reach the bottom, the large maple tree anchoring the corner of the field erupts with a racket of birds. The entire tree is covered with them, and they scream and caw and flap as loudly as a roaring stadium. I stand and watch them for a long time, mesmerized by the great movement and sound. Then, all at once, the tree rushes with wings and the flock takes off, sailing out over the field, banking left, then right, and off behind the church, gone. When I return to my room, the phone is ringing. It's Julia, who asks me to be the godfather of her first child, Kate, who will be born just after I return to New York.

At night I hear the wind scream between the buildings and rattle the windows. I hear shouting down the hall and wonder whether my door will burst open, as it did on the first night, when a dark-haired girl dropped to her knees in the doorway and asked if I was God. I watch the space under my door and see light happen from the other side. Sometimes it is faint, other times bright, then nothing.

In that room, I sit in a chair and feel lighter than I have ever felt— relieved, an impossible weight lifted—until faces begin to appear like fireworks. They keep coming, one after the other—they belonged to my life once, I think—and I feel, sharply, the anger and grief and disappointment and scorn I imagine they hold. I feel heavy again in that chair and sometimes I sit there for hours. I pace my room and leave messages on cell phones and voice mails. Some call back, some never do. I crouch on my knees and pray. For help. For a way through this. For forgiveness. I think of one of my favorite poems and see the predictions it held. I remember my life, how it all mattered so much once, and then not at all. I remember the last lines of a book I believed I understood. *When it feels like the end of the world, it never is.* I knead these words like a rosary and write them in letters and speak them over the phone and into the wind in that field. I lose faith in them, but pray they are true. They are.

I remember all the cabdrivers and hotel employees, dealers, and addicts. The ones who prickled with disgust, fear, or ecstasy, and the ones who said in the same gentle tone that everything would work out, that it would all be okay. I wonder who they thought they were talking to, who it was they saw, who they were. There are things that will always puzzle me—the conversations, the great ballet of taxis and cars, government agents and cops, the JCPenneys—that I will never be able to see clearly enough to distinguish truth from delusion. With these things, these memories, I am only able to remember what they looked like, how they sounded, how it felt. I remember looking out from the balcony of the Gansevoort Hotel that morning. All those people strolling, impossibly, at five a.m.; the Town Cars and the words written on cards that I will always wonder about and often think I should look up to find some meaning in but never do. I remember the seagulls wheeling in great arcs above the river. There were so many.

There is a time, much later, when I imagine what it was like for everyone else, those who were by blood, accident, or inclination involved. Those who were wounded, who wounded. The former came first and fiercest: the employees at the agency who lost their jobs; the writers I represented who depended on me and had to scramble to find new agents; family; friends; Kate. Noah. At first I'm consumed with shame and guilt and regret, but slowly, with the help of kindred spirits, these feelings evolve, are still evolving, into something less self-concerned. The landscape of the latter, with the daily help of those same kindred spirits, is journeyed into. Much remains a frontier.

I wonder what it was like for my father. How the hours I remember from my childhood were for him. What worry he knew. How that drive back from the doctor in Boston went for him. And after. What did he think after the car doors slammed shut and I'd disappeared into the house? Where did he go? To his den to pour himself a Scotch? Around the side of the house to pee in the pachysandra? Or did he stay in the garage and listen to the cooling engine tick down, the tread of footfalls above him in the kitchen. How long might he have stayed there? Did he worry that he'd taken the wrong tack? Been too tough? Too harsh? How would his father have handled it? How much of that man could he even remember? Nineteen years old, when his father died, was a long time ago. He was in college then, planning to join the navy and fly. Fly away from Boston. Jets, cargo planes, it didn't matter—just take flight. How far away did nineteen feel to him that day? How far six? Six years old. What did he know about six-year-old boys? How frightened was he? What didn't he do that day in order to drive his boy to Boston from Fairfield County, Connecticut? What bills didn't get paid? What lawn didn't get mowed? What small plane didn't get fixed or flown in order to do what he thought might help this boy, this boy of his who danced like someone had set him on fire every time he peed? This same boy the doctor said had nothing wrong with him. What the hell was he supposed to do? Wasn't he supposed to be firm? Isn't that how children learned? Wasn't that how men were with their boys?

I wonder if he worried like this. Or did he simply believe that whatever was broken could be fixed by force, that something bent could be hammered straight.

I return to New York and find a small, bright studio with a terrace, and from every corner of the place, I'm able to see the Empire State Building. I kiss someone on the Fourth of July, a friend who becomes more, and he loans me money to afford that place. I sell a photograph I had purchased years before, and with that money and the borrowed money, I am able to live in New York, not work for the first time since I was a teenager, and find, with help, a way to get through the days and nights without escaping them. Gradually, mornings become merely mornings, not panic-stricken hours managing the consequences of not coming home before daybreak, and evenings aren't spent imagining excuses and schemes to get through the next day. Days are just days, not stages where I'm choreographing some complicated piece of theater—the lights, the lines, the costumes—in order to control the outcome, protect myself, get what I think I need.

Returning to publishing doesn't seem possible. It feels like a scorched field that can no longer hold life. But I am wrong. A woman I met once at a party, years before, calls and asks me to lunch, and at that lunch she offers me a job. She talks about courage and no new damage and we eat and drink coffee and it feels like home. The first days back are terrifying, but not in the same way as before. I don't worry about being a fraud or being found out, as I had for all those years. I show up at that office representing one writer—Jean, who, when I told her I was going back to work, wrote her very established agent to say she was switching her representation. Walking through the shiny doors of the agency that day, I somehow trust that if it turns out to be my last one, and she my last client, I will be fine—that the sky won't fall, that it's just not meant to be. It turned out that day was not my last. I'm still in that same office, and have other clients to keep Jean company.

For a long time, I will hear Noah's despairing voice pleading with me, so many times—from behind closed doors, across tables, through phone lines. I will remember every night at the Knickerbocker, every extra drink I snuck when he went to the bathroom. I will remember his coming out to Oregon for family week, standing in the parking lot in his gray snap-front jacket and beard, looking so clean and honest and faithful and loving. I will remember how grateful I was that he never left me. I will remember how his beautiful hands pulled me up that last time and how I fell away from them — finally, because I had to — and moved through the doorway, alone.

In the year before I go back to work, I call my father at least a few times a week, often in the morning as I walk along the Hudson River in a lush park I had, before, not even known was there. We talk, for the first time in many years, and each time, I'm amazed. The very first time we speak is when I'm still in White Plains. The phone rings in my room, I answer, and he is on the line. *Willie,* he says, after a while, *I'm sorry.* He tells me everything he remembers and I listen, quiet, and grateful that I hadn't made it all up. I tell him that my being in rehab is not his fault, that my boyhood struggles did not cause what happened, merely shaped it. Time stops during that phone call; I want it to be over and also never to end.

That October, he asks me to fly in his Cessna from Connecticut to Maine. The small airport is just down the road from where we lived, a few minutes from my high school. I had forgotten how loud small planes are, how light, and how confident my father is in them. His hands glide with easy purpose over the same gadgets and knobs and lights and flaps he handled when I was a boy, and all of it is just as mysterious, just as unknowable. We take off in a field that is also a runway. We shudder along in the way little airplanes do and then, in the split second that always feels as if fairy dust has been sprinkled, we leave the earth, lift quickly, higher and higher, above the towns and schools and the colorful rot of autumn. The roar of the engine and wind make talk impossible. A pile of maps rests in my lap. Side by side, tossing in air, above the fields and hills and roads where everything happened, we are silent.

The Hollow

He's almost two. Walking now. Chubby and cheerful, eats everything put in front of him and always wants more. He disappears
into daydreams and collapses into fits of uncontrollable laughter.
His sister is skinny and fair, his father is dark and smells of smoke,
and his mother is every color in between, every shape, every smell.
She has the bluest eyes. She plants flowers, plants them everywhere—in rock gardens that rise from the lawn into the woods,
along walkways, in pots that sit on windowsills, on steps.

She is planting flowers now, and he is nearby, on a blanket littered
with toys. They are on the lawn behind the house, just at its edge,
where it rises and descends into what they call the hollow, a low,
damp bowl of lawn spotted with outcroppings of granite ledge.
Along the ridge and down along the hollow, there are thickets of
blueberry bushes and, behind those, the woods.

His mother calls to him in her singsong way from behind an enormous straw hat. The two cats sit at the edge of the blanket and
watch him. He can hear them purring and he wants to hold them
and somehow bring their softness and their sounds closer, into
him. He reaches for them and they meow, slink patiently away,
and settle in the just-far-enough-away grass.

Past the cats the dark green lawn stretches toward the woods.
These things, these places, the whole world beyond the immediate
perimeter of his blanket and his mother, have only lately begun to
occur to him. Each new miracle hatches alive, new and beguiling.
A bee, a plane flying overhead, an anthill at the edge of the blanket, a great wind roaring in the trees. He wants to see it all at once
and right away.

This is the first summer he can walk. The first summer he can
move himself closer to what he wants. Away from what he does
not want. He is still in diapers but those will be gone soon. He
looks up past the little ridge, beyond the hollow, and sees a great
shimmering of branches and leaves rising from an army of tree
trunks. A gust of wind sends the leaves into hysterics, and he hears
the sound, like water thundering from the faucet when his mother
draws him a bath. But this new sound is greater, wilder, more
thrilling than anything he's ever heard.

His mother, in her flowers, hums a song, swats flies from her face.
He stands up from the blanket and rocks on his dimpled legs. A

blast of wind in the trees stirs up another momentary chaos. His heart races, and he tilts toward the tree line on the other side of the hollow and begins to move. The swooping birds, the cresting green lawn, the buzzing insects, the tufts of seed and summer flotsam drifting in slow motion through the air, the blueberry bushes at the edge of the wood — all of it dazzles before him. Every gorgeous new inch of it beckons as he walks faster, more deliberately, faster still, until walking isn't fast enough and he begins to run. He's running now, to the top of the lawn, toward the creaking branches, the flashing leaves, the avalanche of sound.

He clears the ridge and, all at once, the slope on the other side is steeper than he expects. His legs whirl beneath him and he struggles not to fall. He's running faster than he has ever run before, and for a second he feels a distance between himself and his body — as if one has departed from the other and is a witness to its new speed and not its cause. The lawn, his legs, his body all blur below him, and he begins to let go, to allow the momentum to carry him.

A great wind pounds through the hollow and he feels on the verge of flight, that the earth will release him and he will surge beyond the lawn, over the vegetable garden and swing set, to the treetops. His mother calls out from somewhere. She is shouting his name, but her voice is small and known and behind him now. Everything that once held his attention, every little and large thing he has remembered, disappears as he races ahead, legs pumping under him, air rushing at his face, terror and wonder bursting from his small heart.

As he careens down the slope, another first, another new magic: calm, like peaceful lightning, flashing through his rioting limbs, stilling every streaking inch of him, caressing him in the half seconds before he stumbles, before he scrapes his elbows and knees and face on the outcropping of granite ledge. Before he wails with shock and his mother descends on him in a flap of hat and tears. Before she gathers him into her and he forgets his fright because he is held in familiar arms that smell of potting soil and flowers. Before all this, a God-kissed, God-cursed calm, debuting at the zenith of his velocity, the peak of his want — a moment that's over before it's even a moment, the one he will scrape his skin hundreds of times to recapture. Before, despite, and because of all the things he senses await him, he leans, then leaps, into the wind, away.

Acknowledgments

Great Force Who Came: Jennifer Rudolph Walsh; Perfect Editor: Pat Strachan; Brilliant Publishers: Michael Pietsch, David Young; Wise Comrade: Robin Robertson; Right Hand: Matt Hudson; Beloved Team: Jonathan Galassi, Nick Flynn, John Bowe, Jill Bialosky, Christopher Potter; Care and Counsel: Adam McLaughlin, David Gilbert, Lili Taylor, Cy O'Neal, Julia Eisenman, James Lecesne, Chris Pomeroy, Laura Gersh, Courtney Hodell, Eliza Griswold, Lee Brackstone, Lisa Story, Roger Manix, Susannah Meadows, Ally Watson, Monica Martin; Love: Jean Stein; Hero: Kim Nichols; My Enduring Family: Mom, Dad, Kim, Lisa, Sean, Matt, Ben, Brian.

About the Author

Bill Clegg is a literary agent in New York. *Portrait of an Addict as a Young Man* is his first book.